CECIL KUHNE is a travel writer specialising in adventure travel, particularly whitewater rafting and mountain trekking. He has travelled on every continent except Antarctica, and has a particular fondness for the Himalaya, the Andes and the Brooks Range in Alaska. His travel articles have appeared in various magazines and newspapers in the United States.

A summer spent working as a raft guide in the Grand Canyon inspired his first article on river-running twenty-five years ago. Since then he has served as contributing editor to various canoeing, kayaking and whitewater-rafting magazines, and written nine books on the subject. A fifth-generation Texan, he practises law in Dallas – except, that is, when he is travelling or writing, which he greatly prefers.

LONELY PLANET . . .

# ON THE EDGE

Adventurous Escapades from
around the World

**Edited by Cecil Kuhne**
**foreword by Tony Wheeler**

LONELY PLANET PUBLICATIONS
Melbourne • Oakland • London • Paris

Lonely Planet . . . On the Edge: Adventurous Escapades from around the World

Published by Lonely Planet Publications
   Head Office:    PO Box 617, Hawthorn, Vic 3122, Australia
   Branches:      150 Linden Street, Oakland, CA 94607, USA
                    10a Spring Place, London NW5 3BH, UK
                    1 rue Dahomey, 75011, Paris, France

Published 2000

Printed by The Bookmaker International Ltd.
Printed in China

Map by Natasha Velleley
Designed by Margaret Jung

National Library of Australia Cataloguing in Publication Data

On the edge: adventurous escapades from around the world

ISBN 1 86450 222 3.

1. Adventure and adventurers. 2. Voyages and travels.
I. Kuhne, Cecil, 1952– . (Series: Lonely Planet journeys.)

910.4

Introduction, selection and notes on contributors © Cecil Kuhne 2000
Map © Lonely Planet 2000
Additional copyright information appears on pp. ix–xii
LONELY PLANET and the Lonely Planet logo are trade marks of Lonely
Planet Publications Pty. Ltd.

# CONTENTS

# COPYRIGHT ACKNOWLEDGEMENTS

Coleridge & White Ltd, 20 Powis Mews, London W11 1JN, and Grove/Atlantic, Inc.

DEBORAH SHAPIRO and ROLF BJELKE, excerpt from *Time on Ice: A Winter Voyage to Antarctica*. Copyright © 1998 by Northern Light Inc. Published by International Marine/Ragged Mountain Press, a division of The McGraw-Hill Companies. Reproduced with permission of The McGraw-Hill Companies.

JOE SIMPSON, excerpt from *Touching the Void* (p. 157). Copyright © 1989 by Joe Simpson. Reprinted by permission of HarperCollins Publishers, Inc, and Jonathan Cape.

STUART STEVENS, excerpt from *Night Train to Turkistan: Modern Adventures along China's Ancient Silk Road*. Copyright © 1988 by Stuart Stevens. Used by permission of Grove/Atlantic, Inc.

MIKE STROUD, excerpt from *Shadows on the Wasteland*. Copyright © 1993 by Mike Stroud. Reproduced by permission of Jonathan Cape and Overlook Press.

PAUL THEROUX, excerpt from *The Old Patagonian Express: By Train through the Americas*. Copyright © 1979 by Cape Cod Scriveners Co. Reprinted by permission of Penguin UK and Houghton Mifflin Company. All rights reserved.

Thanks are also due to Denise Bontoft, the Random House Library and Archive; Brian Halley, the Tessa Sayle Literary Agency; Emily Hayward, Fourth Estate; Catherine Usher, Bloomsbury Publishing; and the Society of Authors (UK) for assistance in tracing copyright owners.

TONY WHEELER

# FOREWORD

**R**IDE ENOUGH third world buses and trains, eat enough questionable meals, swing your leg across enough motorcycles, walk enough mountain trails, cross enough dodgy borders . . . in short, travel far enough and you're bound to have the odd moment on the edge. I *do* manage to rack up rather more than the average number of travelling days each year, and inevitably some of the trips are to places you could call, well, edgy – so it's hardly surprising that I have had some opportunities to muse about mortality. In fact after, 'what's your favourite place,' the travel question I have to field most often is, 'what's the most dangerous thing that's ever happened to you?'

Oh sure, I've bumped into the odd shark when scuba diving, I've flown on some planes whose maintenance standards I'd rather not think about, and there was that time I found myself in the Turkish bath in Syria on ladies day, but frankly my most frightening travel moments have all been in common or garden buses or taxis. In fact, Tom Miller's tale of an Ecuadorian 'bus plunge' struck a chord because it was on that very same bus-plunge-prone road that my wife Maureen and I decided that arriving on time was no longer relevant, that sacrificing half the bus fare wasn't even very important – that simply getting out of that clearly doomed vehicle was the only answer. Our children were aged two and four at the time, and we decided that if they were going to see three and five we had to abandon that bus. Immediately.

Tom's story from *The Panama Hat Trail* may have seemed

eerily familiar but many of the stories in *On the Edge* are simple reminders that I have led a very sheltered life. A safe, quiet, unexciting, stress free, in fact, rather boring life. A squint through my backyard telescope will probably be as close as I'll ever get to Buzz Aldrin's momentous first steps on the moon, recalled in *Men from Earth*. Sailing in tropical waters is quite exciting enough for me; I have no intention of even imagining emulating Deborah Shapiro and Rolf Bjelke's yachting foray to Antarctica in *Time on Ice.*

At times the dangers of being out there are all too evident. Joe Simpson's tale of a mountaineering accident in *Touching the Void* is simply horrific, but sometimes it's the sheer uncertainty which takes the tale right to the edge. Geoffrey Moorhouse's adventure with a very spooked desert guide in *The Fearful Void* was more comedy than terror. Or perhaps it wasn't? David Ewing Duncan's misadventures in *From Cape to Cairo* were definitely edging towards the fear and alarm end of the scale, although here again uncertainty about intentions added a comic slant to the situation. Fortunately Zambia is a much less paranoid country these days.

Jeff Greenwald's Arab Gulf to Pakistan boat trip in *The Size of the World* was also plagued by uncertainty, as only ship trips beset with insurmountable communication problems can be. Are these guys totally incompetent or completely in control? The latter it turns out on this occasion, but I've been all at sea and at sea on what felt like very similar boats.

*Full Tilt,* Dervla Murphy's account of her epic Ireland-to-India bicycle trip in the 1960s, has probably inspired more distance on two wheels than a hundred Tours de France. Her trip up to Bamian in Afghanistan combines uncertainty, discomfort and an inopportune puncture, but the conclusion, in the decrepit 'Luxury, Grade A' Bamian Hotel, had a decidedly familiar feel. The spitting run-down-image of that dilapidated hotel exists today, forty years later, in plenty of places in the world, western Tibet for example. Similarly, Stuart Steven's nightmare bus ride in *Night Train to Turkistan* was also uncomfortably familiar; India has plenty of incarnations of that bus from hell.

The kayak expeditions appealed simply because they were not

big budget extravaganzas. No NASA launch vehicle was necessary for Maria Coffey to set off down India's holy Ganges with *A Boat in our Baggage* but the experiences were as off-the-planet as only Indian adventures can be, and Maria perfectly captures that comedy routine of Indian encounters. In a very different climate, Chris Duff's sea kayak took him past Ireland's ominous Cliffs of Moher in *On Celtic Tides*. Now *that* I've seen from the opposite perspective, walking along the clifftops on a stormy Irish summer morning and climbing down them on a rather sunnier and calmer afternoon. But to paddle by them, looking up at those towering, menacing ramparts, well that must have really been an edgy experience.

Two feet were all the transport Graham Mackintosh required for his marathon walk around the coast of Baja California. *Into a Desert Place* was clearly, as this extract reveals, tough, worrying, scary, but immensely satisfying. In *One for the Road,* Tony Horwitz's hitchhike to Coober Pedy – the inspiration for the post nuclear holocaust city in the final Mad Max extravaganza – is a reminder that in the Australian outback merely being there can provide an on-the-edge experience. And a whole lot of surrealistic fun.

Other adventurers sail, raft, cycle, dog sled, lose things (from their modesty in Africa to a faithful dog in Australia) or even, in Dea Birkett's *Serpent in Paradise* encounter, fight off a randy Chief Steward in a cargo ship's cold room. Yet Paul Theroux's El Salvador versus Mexico soccer match in *The Old Patagonian Express* shows that even attending a sports event can be challenging. Clearly in Central America football is a whole lot more than just a sport: in fact, a few years previously, the brief 'Football War' did erupt between El Salvador and Honduras after a game at the same location.

ARCTIC
OCEAN

EUROPE

ASIA

CHRIS
DUFF

BRIAN
HALL

KATHERINE
KIZILOS

STUART
STEVENS

DERVLA
MURPHY

WILLIAM
DALRYMPLE

MARIA
COFFEY

GEOFFREY
MOORHOUSE

AFRICA

JEFF
GREENWALD

MARK
JENKINS

RORY
NUGENT

KEVIN
KERTSCHER

ERIC
HANSEN

RICK
RIDGEWAY

DAVID
EWING
DUNCAN

ATLANTIC
OCEAN

INDIAN
OCEAN

ROBYN
DAVIDSON

AUSTRALIA

TONY
HORWITZ

SOUTHERN
OCEAN

ANTARCTICA

MIKE
STROUD

BUZZ ALDRIN
ALASTAIR SCOTT
NORTH AMERICA
TED CONOVER
GRAHAM MACKINTOSH
PICO IYER
ATLANTIC OCEAN
CENTRAL AMERICA
PACIFIC OCEAN
PAUL THEROUX
REDMOND O'HANLON
TOM MILLER
OCEANIA
JOE SIMPSON
SOUTH AMERICA
DEA BIRKETT
WHIT DESCHNER
ERIC NEWBY
DEBORAH SHAPIRO & ROLF BJELKE

## CECIL KUHNE

# INTRODUCTION

*C*.S. LEWIS once noted that 'To have lost the taste for marvels and adventures is no more a matter for congratulation than losing our teeth, our hair, our palate, and finally, our hopes.' Lewis is not alone; a whole industry has sprung up around the pursuit of adventure. There are now legions of people throughout the world who are kayaking across perilous ocean waves, trekking over vast ice caps, hiking through dense jungles and bicycling down remote valleys. In most cases these individuals are guided by competent outfitters who make sure their clients are well fed and comfortable enough to justify their considerable fees.

But *true* travel adventure travel is different. Riskier. Wilder. Often alone . . . and without a safety net.

Adventure travel can also be described simply as a poorly planned vacation. You suddenly find yourself in some far-flung spot without the usual supports, conveniences and backups of modern life. There are no cell phones or emergency rescue services. No support groups. No law and order. Which is exactly what makes this kind of travel more interesting – and more compelling.

Adventure travel can be nasty, brutish and short. And that's only the good days. Officials of various echelons can lead you into some pretty unpleasant exchanges, and the people you meet in the street can cast you deep into cultural clashes. Then you have the situations presented by the natural world: mountain climbing, where one false step means a very nasty 300-foot free fall; a storm at sea, where the sails on the ship hang together on a single thread; the unforgiving desert, where the relentless sun renders life totally barren.

Fortunately, there are many fine authors willing to share the excitement, the fears, the joys and the pain of their journeys. For the past twenty years, I have collected books of adventure travel, and my entire garage is lined with the memoirs of such escapades. My review of these books – and many more besides – has been an exciting and challenging undertaking. It wasn't easy to distil the list for this anthology, but what you have before you is, I believe, the best of the best.

The assembled stories span all seven continents (and even the moon), and range from a trek across the Sahara to a sail through Antarctica, from encountering giant South American spiders to the loss of a canine travelling companion. Global boundaries are no impediment to the adventures one can collect if armed with the right attitude. In fact, you can have them in your own neighbourhood if you look closely enough and keep an open mind. Our authors have all met travel writer Mark Jenkins' rigorous definition: 'Adventure means embracing both serendipity and disaster, and it happens when you – yes you, no one else – suddenly have to solve a problem in which the wrong move can have dire consequences.'

The old adage that truth is stranger than fiction is certainly true of adventure travel books. Reading these accounts, you realise that there is no way anyone could have dreamed up such things in their imagination. Yet the writers are amazingly unassuming about their adventures. There is no braggadocio – such exhilarating travel experiences, it seems, are humbling ones – and there are no travel bores. Such engaging tales never cease to fascinate.

These itinerant souls do, however, have one thing in common: they went, in spite of what others advised was sheer lunacy. These are infectious stories that I hope will incite you to push your own boundaries. Good reading and bon voyage . . . without the safety net!

# AFRICA

# MARK JENKINS

# TO TIMBUKTU

ONE MORNING I am on a straight stretch of river ahead of the others. I am not thinking about anything, just paddling. Moving my boat through the warm water. The river is dun, the banks verdant, the sky pallid blue.

For no reason I turn my head and glance over my shoulder.

Mike and John are backpaddling wildly, trying to shove their boats in reverse. Rick is halfway between me and them. He is perhaps forty feet behind me, gliding serenely through the water. To his right is a rippling wedge moving directly for him. Bulbous nose and slick eyes and then nothing for fifteen feet until the ridge of a notched, swaying tail.

Mike has stowed his paddle and is scrambling for his gun.

I drop my paddle and jerk on the lanyard. The gun pops into my hand. I swing around in my cockpit and brace my elbows on the combing and try to compose myself.

Rick is almost dawdling. The croc is coming right at him but he is not speeding up or slowing down, he is paddling languidly, now and again turning his head to watch the croc swimming toward him.

Mike has his gun in his hands and his shoulders blocked. His boat is sliding soundlessly toward Rick. John is behind Mike, frozen.

Twisted around, the 9-millimetre steady in both hands, consciously controlling my breathing, my arms slowly moving with the croc, watching Mike out of the corner of my eye with Rick between us and the crocodile going straight for him, I suddenly see what will happen. We will both fire at once and it will be like some slapstick shtick. I will kill Mike and Mike will kill me, and the croc, seeing his chance, will drag Rick under.

Rick is relaxed. I don't know if he's even noticed the rest of us. The croc is closing in. Thirty feet, twenty feet, ten feet . . .

*Blup.*

The croc vanishes.

I wait, holding mortally still, finger on the trigger, aiming, expecting a primeval salamander to surge from the placid water, jaws clapping, teeth gnashing, and in one clean chomp take Rick's head right off.

Nothing. The river is blank.

Rick paddles past me, turns his head, and smiles.

We decide to travel in a convoy. Single file, a hundred feet between each kayak, the gunboats in positions one and three.

We make up signals: paddle held horizontally overhead with hands equally spaced – stop. Paddle held vertically overhead – caution. Paddle held vertically overhead and waved – emergency, come quick. Paddle held horizontally overhead with blade extended to port or starboard – something is over there, look. Paddle held horizontally overhead and vigorously stroking the air – paddle hard, now.

Who knows if they will help.

Mike and I alternate as point man. We both want it. It is the chance to play scout.

Now that we are seriously looking for crocs, we see them. They are seldom out in the body of the river. They stay in the shade along the banks, their greasy green eyes peeping through the drowned trees.

When you are hunting, you don't look for shapes or colours. If you do, everything is an animal. Logs look like bodies, branches like claws, sticks like tails. Instead you learn to let your eyes ride over the landscape on their own. They will search for you. It is not form or hue they will pick out, but motion. Your eyes spot movement instinctively, even the breath of movement, and hold on it like a pointing dog until your mind sees what they see. It is evolutionary. The human nose is a joke, the ears barely adequate; but the *eyes*, the eyes of a human are the eyes of a predator.

It feels good to be hunting. The moment you begin to hunt, you cease being the hunted. It is a complete metamorphosis. To hunt is to believe in your own power, to believe you will win and not lose. It's a worthwhile feeling even when it doesn't work and you are defeated. And we all are defeated, just not by what we think will defeat us.

That night the sides of the river are so overgrown it's difficult to find a place to dock. It gets dark and we finally have to pull off right where we are. We thread through the sunken trees, jump into the black water, haul our boats through the mud, and tie up.

We tramp down a spot in a mangle of ferns and set up the tents by rote. John whips dinner together, something invisible at the bottom of the pot; then we repair to our separate tents like old couples. For a few minutes the beams of our headlamps roam the surface of our homes, seeking bugs. We kill all we can, click off our lights, lie back and sleep.

We wake in the morning with backaches. Lumpy beds and too many hours in the saddle. We move slow, our bodies taking longer to wake up than we do. Mike and John are finished dressing first and wander down to the boats. Rick and I begin to drop our tents, sliding the poles out. Rick has his pants on, his shirt unbuttoned. I'm in shorts, no shirt.

I'm messing with the broken poles of our tent. My back is turned and I hear Rick start slapping – *thap, thap, thap* – but I'm not paying attention. Then he starts cursing, and Rick doesn't curse, and then a low rumble comes over me and Rick begins to

7

screech. It's a piercing cry, a sound I have never heard a man make before. I spin around to find Rick twirling like a dervish slapping and screeching and then he is flying toward me passing me and I'm running now too not knowing what is happening until the black cloud is all around me stinging me and Rick is already in the water and John is in the water and I'm diving in.

I am underwater swimming. I can feel the creatures fluttering in my flesh like thorns. I swim out where the current is and come to the surface and grab the limbs to keep from being swept away and start pulling myself back in toward shore.

Rick and John are there. Only their heads stick above the water. As I come in, John shouts, 'Duck!' and their heads disappear and then I see the patrol of bees and go under myself but start giggling and have to come up.

Seconds later Rick and John pop to the surface.

'Looked like they got you bad,' says Rick.

'Did they get you?'

'Mostly on the head.'

'Duck!'

Beneath the water we are safe. It is our carapace. But we can only hold our breath for so long. We come up together.

'Where's Mike?'

John points down the bank. Mike didn't go into the water. He's standing stock-still, his hands clamped over his face, bees crawling all over him.

'Mike, you all right?'

'Just dandy.' His voice is muffled.

Bees are everywhere. They are sending out patrol after patrol looking for us. We go under, hold our breath, come up.

'Rick, what happened?'

'Did you see the hive?'

'No.'

'We camped right under it. Thing's big as a cage ball. It was hanging from that tree. I accidentally jabbed it with a tent pole.'

We start laughing but our laughter gets garbled because we have to go under again.

When we come up, John whispers, 'Look at the boats.'

Our kayaks are carpeted with a fibrillating mass. We have been living on oranges and our nylon cockpits are soaked with juice.

Rick says, 'We'll just have to wait it out.'

We've been in the water half an hour when Mike moves. He takes one very slow step, then stops, his hands still over his face. Two minutes later he takes another step. In twenty minutes he has gone twenty feet.

The roar is subsiding now. The patrols are gone but our boats are still unapproachable. Rick and I are still hiding out in the water. John has pulled his shirt up over his head and has started moving toward the boats, staying as much under water as possible.

Mike is taking one slow step at a time along the bank. He has removed his hands from his face. Bees land, crawl across his cheeks, along his lips, over his eyelids, then fly away. We wait and watch.

We have been in the water over an hour when Mike reaches the boats. The decks are still heavy with bees. With a bare hand he slowly wipes the bees off the rear hatch. They plop into the mud in a yellow clump. He opens the hatch, pulls out his cap with the bug net, gently wipes the bees off his face and neck, puts the cap on and drops the net. He reaches back inside the hatch, lifts out a pair of leather gloves, slides his hands inside. He is safe. He stands up, turns to us and waves with both hands.

'Hi, guys.'

We are incredulous. 'Did you get stung at all?'

'Nope.' He shakes his head and grins. 'So, guys,' suddenly he starts coughing with laughter, 'How's the water?'

'What? What is it?'

'Forget about the crocs?'

We boat all day hardly speaking. The banks close in and we skim through dim passageways, peeping into the shadows.

When the jungle is all around us like this, almost on top of us, it doesn't feel as if we're moving downstream. It feels as if we're moving upstream, up into someplace dark and nepenthean.

We all jump when a troop of monkeys begins screaming. They are very large monkeys. They resemble furry, evil children. They screech and show us their sharp teeth and thrash through the trees trying to chase us away.

In the late afternoon we spot a dugout along the bank and pull off. It is filled with mud. There is a trail leading into the bush but it is so indistinct we don't know if it was made by humans or animals. We follow it hoping it will lead us to a village but it just burrows on and on until we have to turn around.

That night a heavy fog settles over us. In the morning we huddle together and eat the last of our food. Bananas turned bitter, hunks of cassava left in the pot from the night before. We whisper instead of talk as though the fog were a net that could drop on us if we raised our voices. John thinks we could make Faranah today. Rick hopes so. Mike doesn't think we can but that's only because he doesn't want to.

We load our boats in the thick mist and slide them like spoons into the blood of the water. We plan to travel in convoy but the fog separates us immediately. At first we call out to one another; then we stop, letting each of us find his own way. We can't get lost. We're on a river, not an ocean.

I let the current carry me, my prow spreading the petals of whiteness and pulling me through as if I were passing into the depths of a flower. I listen to the small joyful sounds my paddle makes upon the water.

Once I stop my arms and coast, the paddle clasped before me. I want to listen to the sound of my boat slipping through the water. I think I can hear it, but perhaps not.

Sometimes I think I see a shadow glancing through the void beside me. It comes and goes. Only when the fog begins to lift do I realise it is Michael. We have been parallel for a long time. We are bending in toward each other when he raises his paddle and points downriver.

There's something out there, a phantom. We line up and paddle together not knowing what it is we are pursuing. Then the veil lifts.

It is a man. He is lean, knotted with muscle, putting his shoulders into the pole. He is sending his dugout over the water like a gondolier with a message. Before we can get his attention he vanishes into the reeds.

We follow him. We find his boat but he is gone. We scramble up the bank and run through a tunnel of grass. At the end of the tunnel there is an opening.

Inside the enclosure there will be five blind men. The boatman and an old man with grey hair and three others. At their feet will be a drawing in the dirt. A circle with wavy lines inside it.

The men will be mute and rigid as animals. Rough dusty legs of muscle and bodies of muscle and inscrutable faces.

When we ask them questions, they will not respond to us. They will be blank. Human pillars supporting the weight of the African sky. Mike and I will go back to our boats. Out on the river we will slide into an eddy to wait for Rick and John and wonder why the old man drew a picture in the sand that none of them could see.

But it was not drawn for them. It was drawn for us.

On every journey there is something waiting for you. Something specific. When you find it, you will think it just happened to be there, but in fact it was there only for you. It is not a coincidence. If you had not found it, it would not have been there.

GEOFFREY MOORHOUSE

# THE FEARFUL VOID
## Across the Implacable Sahara,
## a Man Goes in Search of Himself

THE OASIS of Tidjikja, in many ways, resembled some place out of Conrad rather than the writings of P. C. Wren. It straddled the wadi we had seen from afar, with humpbacked tents pitched among palm trees on the south bank and rows of mud houses standing back from the north bank. On the rare occasions when the wadi flowed with water, there would be a river here, two hundred yards wide, dividing these two halves of the village. Now, in the fourth year of the drought, there was an expanse of bare sand on which camels sat couched in twos and threes, and across which figures in blue sometimes moved, their heads swathed up to the eyeballs against the dust and wind that constantly swept the wadi from end to end. Even so, the north bank, with its fringe of tiny shops on whose doorsteps men always lounged aimlessly, felt much like a waterfront. The steps dropped deeply into the sand and formed a kind of wharf running the length of a non-existent water's edge. When the men moved a few feet to unhobble a camel and kick it gently into action, it required but a touch of the imagination to see them untying their canoes before paddling off upstream towards the old French fort on the inward bend of the river, now inhabited by the Mauritanian *préfet* and his handful of soldiery. As at Chinguetti, the previous colonial incumbents of this building had placed a great expanse of open ground between themselves and the native inhabitants of the oasis.

We lodged in a room shared by four other men and a small boy while, outside in a dusty yard, a tent was occupied by the women and girls of the household. The room had once been whitewashed, but now its walls were filthy and flaked, its floor was a rubble of dust and date stones, and the only light came in through the doorway. In Europe one would have described it as a cow shed, but here it was a welcome shelter from heat and cold alike. The men came and went about their business of carrying other people's goods upon a couple of donkeys, while the women cooked and interminably pounded meal in wooden bowls with great staves which were bulbous and smooth at each end. Droves of children came from all the neighbourhood to peer through the doorway at the strange creature within, then rushed off shrieking *'Nasrani! Nasrani!'* in voices which suggested they had just clapped eyes on the original bogey man.

I sat there, happy at first to be inactive, but with a growing sense of strain as I wrote, read, played chess and acted as host to more flies than I could ever recall having seen in one place. At Sidi Ahmed's house in Atar they had swarmed thickly between the bakery and the adjacent midden; on the march one often shouldered epaulettes of flies which presumably preferred the rhythm of a man to that of a camel; but here there were so many that large patches of the floor were sometimes obscured by their crawling bodies – and I was one day able to count thirty-seven moving up and down my motionless arm.

We had been there for twenty-four hours when young Mahomed rose to his feet, wrapped his howli round his head and announced, 'I'm off.' We went to help him load the camels in the lane outside and then, with a handshake and a big grin, he set out on the lonely way back to Chinguetti – with no moon, in a high and cold wind, out into the black wilderness as casually as though he were strolling down Tottenham Court Road for the last Tube train to Waterloo. Mohamed ould Moctar ould Hmeida showed no such anxiety to be on his way again, and I began to have grave misgivings about his reliability. The day after young Mahomed had departed, he said he'd found someone who would sell us two camels for £150. When I reminded him that in Atar he had vowed that the very finest beast could be obtained here for a maximum of £60, he said the majority of camels had left only the week before for sale in Atar. Next day he invited me to take a look at a good bull he thought we might purchase.

It was hobbled down on the edge of the wadi and, as we approached, a crowd gathered, sensing an impending sale. A dozen men and boys began to examine the animal knowingly, as though they were of a mind to buy it themselves, pulling down its lower lip to see its teeth and pressing their fists into its hump; one old man lifted its tail offhandedly, then gave it a hard tug, to which the camel paid not the slightest heed. As for Mohamed, he walked round the beast, looked at its teeth, felt its ribs and rubbed the palms of his hands together like a fairground salesman tensely waiting for the first bid in a Dutch auction. It would do, he said, for the £64 its owner wanted. What about the other one? I asked. Ah, that one, he said, was to be found at Rachid and he, Mohamed, would ride this one back there to collect it.

Why the hell, I demanded, had he not taken steps to buy the beast three days before, when we had passed Rachid on the way down from his own tent? Ah, he didn't know then that the camel would be there. For a man on whose doorstep all these animals were variously deployed, this seemed to me a very thin story indeed and I told him so, suspecting that he was now paying me back for my failure to allow him a day longer with his family. Hurt by my bluntness, he accused me of not trusting him. It was half true; my doubts had been growing all the way from Akjoujt. We parted coolly, he taking the remainder of the £150 to complete the transaction.

The next few days were a miserable trial of waiting for him to return. I became irritable with the people around me when I discovered in their yard a sack of sorghum flour which bore the plain inscription 'Donated by the people of the United States to the people of Mauritania. NOT to be sold or exchanged in barter.' I had seen one similar to it in the marketplace of Akjoujt, another trifle of conscience money from the West which had become somebody's bit of graft in the debilitating corruption of the Third World. This family had paid 3,000 francs, about £6, for their flour to a trader in Tidjikja. When I tried to explain the immorality of this commerce, they roared with laughter at my foolishness.

That evening was the first of a sequence in which I was harangued by a pompous young man on the superiority of Islam over all other faiths, on the clarity of its truths, on the sensuous delights that awaited its believers, on the damnation that was in store for all others. He was genuinely puzzled when he discovered that, although I could recite el Fateha and el Shehahda in his own tongue, I could not honestly subscribe to the beliefs embodied in either.

One morning I heard an aircraft descending and watched a small monoplane land on the oasis airstrip half a mile away. Instantly I longed to take flight on it back to Nouakchott, back to Europe, back home to my own people. I wanted to be away from the appalling filth of these surroundings, from the awfulness of this food, from the loneliness of spirit and the increasing alienation I felt wedging me apart from these primitive human beings. I wanted to fly from children who shouted *'Nasrani!'* mockingly at every corner, from adults who slithered deviously from one apparent fiction to another as it suited their purpose.

But another predicament prevented me from taking a single step towards the aircraft and the American who was said to pilot it, towards the collection of prefabricated huts where a Frenchman was in charge of a petrol company's base for desert operations. I knew I did not dare visit the petroliers, for already I had become a hybrid creature, fitting neither the patterns of the desert nor those of Europe. If I walked up to the huts, the two Westerners would doubtless offer me a beer and a good wash, both of which I could well use. But their first reaction would be one of repugnance at my scarecrow appearance and my disagreeable smell; it would not be uttered, but it would flicker for an instant across their faces, enough to stultify me and turn my indifferent French into spluttering gibberish.

I never did meet the petroliers. I lurked around the village until the plane took off again for the west, before I strolled up to the airstrip and sat upon a boulder. A half gale was beginning to drum up out of the desert and plumes of dust were streaming down the gravel of the runway, stinging the eyes like cigarette ash. The first week of December was over, and in London the Christmas shopping crowds would have started to plunge and plunder the length of Oxford Street in a different kind of wilderness. Was A in the middle of that lot, as sick at heart as I was here, in this sand-blasted corner of nowhere? At my present rate of progress it would be nearly the end of January before I reached Tombouctou, when all my calculations had assumed I would complete my first stage soon after New Year's Day.

After almost a week in Tidjikja I was pacing down the airstrip at sunset when I saw a rider leading a second camel at the trot round the edge of the oasis. Mohamed had returned, and so great was my relief at the prospect of moving on again that I told him to keep the change from the camel-buying. Swollen thus with 6,000 francs and the memory, I assumed, of two nights in his tent, he held court before the household that evening, cocky as a sparrow. Next afternoon, he promised, we would leave, after he had attended to one or two small matters of his own.

It was with a mixture of excitement and nervousness that I led my two camels up the lane and into open scrub, while Mohamed exchanged farewells with three women who had appeared as we were about to depart. At last I had my own beasts, I was more the master of my situation than before, and somehow this seemed to be the real beginning of the journey. But I was much in the hands, for the next few weeks, of this tough and truculent little man who had made me wary of his conduct. We had not gone more than five hundred yards before he started to complain that his back was bad; I said I would put some embrocation on it when we made camp.

We had been walking for little more than an hour when Mohamed indicated some succulent trees about a mile off our course and said that we must stop there for the night, because the camels needed feeding. It was only four o'clock, and there were a couple of hours' good travelling time left in the day, but I remembered Monod's advice about grazing and did not demur. We set ourselves down by some large thornbushes and I started to make our evening meal while Mohamed warmed his back in the sun. In Tidjikja I had obtained a kilo of onions, and tonight, I said, we would have some boiled as a blessed relief from rice, dates and meat. As they cooked on the fire, I strolled relaxed round the bushes, happy to feel the tensions of the past week beginning to slide out of my body. Mohamed lay prone on his stomach, chewing his teeth-cleaning stick, brooding silently on my movements.

As the sun began to dip over the horizon, I noticed a couple of men walking in our direction, though on a course that would not run through our camp. One of them carried a very ancient-looking rifle, with a long barrel and an enormous stock, but otherwise there was nothing unusual about them; some time before, three women on donkeys had ridden the same way. The men, deep in conversation and taking not the slightest notice of us, were never within three hundred yards before they disappeared into the dunes behind. Mohamed, however, suddenly became very excited. There was, he said, something odd about the men. Telling me to hide behind a bush, he started to walk back the way we had come, towards a tent which was pitched inside a thorn fence about half a mile away. I stood there, feeling faintly ridiculous, for I could see nothing at all in the men's behaviour that made concealment necessary.

But when Mohamed returned, he was jumpy with agitation. We must get back to Tidjikja at once, he said. The men were going to encircle us behind the dunes and would surely attack us the moment darkness fell. This seemed to me patent nonsense. No one intending attack, I said, would have allowed us to see him, for a start. The men were plainly going to some encampment, as the women had been before them. Not so, said Mohamed; he had checked with the family at the tent and they had vowed that no encampment lay in that direction. I repeated my reasoned argument, but Mohamed dismissed it contemptuously.

'You are a Nasrani, I am a Moslem. You do not understand this country and these people as I do. We must go, quickly. I am not afraid for myself, but I cannot have your blood on my hands.'

My ignorance I had to concede, and he knew it. Hastily, in the gathering gloom, he started to pick up a few portable possessions. We must leave everything else, including the camels, which had wandered off hobbled to browse out of sight. Disgracefully we abandoned our camp, including the lovely onions, which were ready for eating, and started to walk rapidly back to the oasis. I had never seen Mohamed move so fast, striding so hurriedly that he soon left me behind. In the darkness I walked into a bush and swore at him to stop. At that moment a gun fired and our rout was complete.

'They're after us,' he cried, and took to his heels like a rabbit. It was useless, and there was now no time, to tell him that judging by the sound, the gunshot must have been quite a mile away. This was a man who appeared to be very badly shaken by fear while I, stumbling irritably in his wake, felt oddly detached about the whole affair. It was too much like a caricature for me to take it seriously.

DAVID EWING DUNCAN

# FROM CAPE TO CAIRO
## An African Odyssey

IN THE MIDDLE of the second night the Fiat's generator died. The driver, still jolly and talkative, kept going on the deserted highway without headlights in the bright African moonlight, rushing into the darkness at seventy miles per hour. It was an eerie ride, silvery and mysterious, with the usual nightjars diving about, their silhouettes murky against the glowing pavement. Periodically, the engine died and the driver had to rouse the male passengers to stumble out of the bus and push until the engine took. None of the passengers complained. 'What is the point of complaining?' said Phoebe. I told her that in America it was unlikely that paying passengers would get out and push a bus in the middle of the night. 'But why?' she said in disbelief. 'Buses break down. What do they do when this happens? Just sit and wait?'

Early on the third day our crippled bus pulled into Kasama, capital of the northernmost region of Zambia. In the crowded, squalid central market we had to abandon our beloved Fiat to an unsavoury-looking mechanic clutching an old wrench. Jim and I considered bicycling from here to Lake Tanganyika, about two hundred kilometres away. After the warmth of the Fiat the situation seemed less grim in Zambia, and we were anxious to see some of this remote country on the bikes. Besides, Phoebe told us there was a great downhill above the lake, a vertical drop of nearly two thousand feet.

Our optimism about a relaxation of tensions was premature. We didn't realise that Kasama was just about the worst place to be at that moment. A few days earlier a bridge had been blown up by saboteurs. The entire population was roused, expecting any moment an invasion from the south.

As Jim and I discussed our travel plans, a tall man in a powder blue coat asked to see our passports. He was loud and demanding, but said he was not a policeman. As he spoke, a small crowd gathered, but I didn't think much of it. This was a common occurrence in places where eighteen-speed bikes are a curiosity. Yet people did seem unusually serious. They were pressing in so tightly that we were having a hard time getting air.

When we declined to give him our passports, he became hysterical. 'You are South African spies!' he screamed.

'What?' I stammered, feeling a sudden chill.

'Spies! Spies!' he shouted as the crowd pushed in with ugly expressions. They split to let a policeman through. He asked what was happening, and the powder blue man loudly insisted that we were South African spies and must be taken to the police station for questioning. The policeman looked at the people and at us and realised that he was in over his head. Yet he looked at our passports, showed them to the man and attempted to persuade him that there was no reason to arrest us. I admired his courage and professionalism, but a silent, unfathomable pitch of anger had been reached by the people in the Kasama market.

'Those passports can be faked!' bellowed the powder blue man. I put my hand on his shoulder to reassure him. 'We want to be friends,' said Jim.

He angrily slapped me away. I was startled by the intensity of his violence. I was drawn to his eyes, and was horrified to see the extent of his rage. With a shudder I realised this man *hated* me. It was such a powerful emotion being slung at me that I stepped back in dismay. *He hated me*, and there was nothing I could do to change his mind.

The die, it seemed, had been cast, although this was all happening too fast. 'Sir, we are merely travellers,' I was saying, trying to calm the lunatic in powder blue. But as I spoke, the crowd was swelling from dozens to over a hundred and perhaps more.

They scurried from alleys and shanties into the open space of the market. We were becoming a small, Caucasian eye in a hurricane of enraged faces. The policeman fled when the first tentative rocks and sticks began to fly. We held on tightly to our bikes, the nausea of fear welling up in our bellies, our backs against a low wall that provided some protection. 'Spies! Spies! Spies!' shouted the mob.

'Take them to the station!' Powder Blue shouted. I felt hands grabbing me and my bike, lifting me high into the air to carry me across the market to a waiting flatbed truck. A fist punched me in the ribs and someone struck my head.

I was not going to give in easily. As we were lifted into the truck, I squirmed and fought. 'Where are you taking us?' I bellowed. I was as angry as I was frightened. I had some grossly misplaced conviction that this couldn't be happening to me. No, not to *me!* Not a reasonable, fair individual like myself! I sympathised with their fears about South Africa. I loathed apartheid as much as the next fellow. But what did this matter to the mob?

The crowd cheered when we dropped into the truck bed. Enthusiastic members of the mob jumped aboard and I began for the first time to truly panic, realising at the very least I was going to get beaten up. Then, abruptly, a siren blasted the marketplace. Everyone scattered as a police Land Rover rushed through the people. Soldiers armed with automatic rifles deployed around the truck. The would-be lynchers, including Mr Powder Blue, fled into the crowd. I breathed a guarded sigh of relief, never imagining I would welcome the arrival of the Zambian police. Moments later we found ourselves sitting in the Rover and pulling into a fortified police compound. The mob chased us, but stopped at the gate. 'You are safe now, my friends,' said one of the police.

The police compound was yet another remnant of the colonial era. There were two one-storey buildings, one shaped like a U turned on its back, and the other a straight line resting on top of the U like the dictionary symbol for a long vowel. The long building was the jailhouse, the bottom of the U the main booking room, and the rest of the compound was offices, interrogation rooms and toilets. Long ago, the station must have looked like something out of a

Graham Greene novel, complete with tidy gardens, flowers and fresh paint. Yet little of this stodgy Britishness remained. The courtyard gardens were overgrown and filled with heaps of junk, everything from tyres to a rusty engine block. Each object was labelled with a weather-worn 'evidence tag' attached by a wire. The toilets had been clogged for years. One of them had been cemented over. However, I could still see the faded initials of the imperial police painted in large letters on the roof – NRP, Northern Rhodesia Police. After twenty-five years of independence, no one had bothered to paint them over.

Jim and I were led into the commanding officer's office by police dressed in neat if slightly threadbare uniforms. S. M. Nchiminga (the CO) and three colleagues welcomed us to Kasama and asked if we were hurt in the market imbroglio. We told him we were a bit shaken but physically unharmed. We felt relieved by Nchiminga's geniality, and answered several of the usual police questions about our trip.

Nchiminga then turned and whispered to his colleagues, a dour pregnant woman, a sneering detective in a paisley, three-inch-wide tie and a tall, friendly-looking man in what looked like a naval commander's uniform. I leaned over to say something to Jim and Nchiminga screamed loudly for me to shut up. His abruptness startled me. He then shouted an order to a guard by the door.

'Separate them!' he commanded, his friendly demeanour having disappeared.

'But, sir . . .' I said.

'Shut up,' he retorted. Then to the guard: 'Do not let them speak! They shall be interrogated separately. Take them to separate rooms.' Jim, meanwhile, had been taking out eyedrops for his contact lenses, an innocuous act that elicited a fantastic response.

'Stop him!' shouted the detective in the paisley tie. 'He is trying to take poison!' The guards scrambled to grab the villainous drops, nearly tripping over each other in the effort.

'Those drops are for my eyes,' Jim started to explain.

'Silence!' bellowed Nchiminga. 'You are South African spies. You will be held for questioning.'

'South African spies!' I stammered. 'But, but . . . that is non-sense! What proof do you have?'

'Take them!' he shouted.

I was led to a small room and told to sit on a bench, where I was incarcerated most of that first morning. The hours were excruciating. I had nothing to do. It was dark and I had no idea what the hell was going on. I remembered reading somewhere that detainees in an Argentinian prison tried to pass the time by thinking of pleasant things. I thought of Vermont, hikes through thick stands of pine, my wife's embrace, a crackling fire, a glass of wine . . .

As the hours passed, I took each of these thoughts and mentally lined them up like a shell collection so that I could study each memory. Yet they seemed so distant in that bleak room I soon began to despair. Would I see my wife again? My own little paradise in the hills of Vermont? Somehow, I had to learn to shut down my mind, if I planned to remain sane.

POSTSCRIPT: *David Ewing Duncan was imprisoned for several days and then suddenly released by his captors. He considered himself lucky: a Frenchman was held in the same prison with little food or water for six weeks because he couldn't speak English.*

RICK RIDGEWAY

# THE SHADOW OF KILIMANJARO
## On Foot across East Africa

A CROSS THE RIVER a lone baobab stands on a rock outcrop, its great millennial mass skylighted in emblematic isolation. Baobabs live in the coastal belt of East Africa, occurring inland as much as two hundred miles, and now they are becoming more frequent. The Waliangulu consider baobabs the most sacred of trees, believing that they are the abode of spirits, and a very large baobab, with trunks whose girths span up to seventy-five feet, can live for three thousand years and more, making the oldest of these trees perhaps older than the Waliangulu culture itself.

The game trail we follow leads into a grove of thick juvenile doum, and as we weave around the dense fronds that confine our view, Mohamed raises his rifle to the Number One Position, and I turn the video camera to Standby. Mohamed moves slowly forward, craning his neck around each corner, finger on the trigger, and I consider how in a thicket this dense the distance between discovery and disaster has been reduced to something like a single second.

We all sigh in relief as we exit the palm grove and enter a zone of toothbrush bush. Mohamed relaxes into Number Two Position, but I notice his eyes still sweep right and left like radar. Ahead through the bush I hear the almost human call of a baboon – hey-ha! hey-ha! – alerting others that we are approaching. A martial eagle lands in a tree just ahead, and when we are closer I stop to film this great bird with its massive body and dark, hooded head. This eagle is one of the main predators of the little dik-dik, and now the bird sits on a branch and fixes its eye on me as I zoom in. Suddenly I hear Mohamed yelling, *'Mamba! Mamba!'* – Swahili for crocodile – and I quickly lower the camera and see Mohamed, Iain, Danny and the others running through the bush alongside a seven-foot crocodile. I follow just in time to see the reptile slither into the river and disappear, as the others hoot and cry out in surprise.

'It was quite a long way from the river,' Bongo says. 'And it chose a very funny route back to the water. Kind of slow and sluggish, too.'

'Maybe it was cold,' Danny says.

'I don't know. Odd behaviour. Very odd.'

We walk away from the river toward the area where the others flushed the croc from the bush, and Bongo calls out, 'Come, look here.' We walk over to find Bongo stooped down studying the partially eaten carcass of a freshly killed dik-dik. Only its hindquarters remain. Danny and Bongo converse in Swahili with the rangers, then Bongo says to me, 'It appears that the martial eagle you were photographing killed this dik-dik, then the crocodile crawled off the river and was about to steal the dik-dik from the eagle when we happened along.'

In the approximately one hundred years of experience that Bongo, Danny, Iain and the rangers have adding together all their time in Tsavo, no one has ever seen a crocodile steal a kill from an eagle, or even heard of this happening. 'This is very unusual,' Bongo says again.

We continue through a mix of river acacia with the shorter wait-a-bit in the undergrowth and the large hydra-headed doums at river's edge. I hear the mournful call of the blue-naped mousebird, unseen in the overhead branches. I notice a flash of colour at my foot and stoop to pick up a single wing feather from a kingfisher, and it is coloured an electric blue so bright it appears to be internally illuminated. We drop toward a sand-bottom *lugga*. It is still cloudy and humid. Mohamed suddenly jumps back, waving his hand for everyone to freeze. He points excitedly toward the bottom of the gully, and for a second I don't see anything, but then I make out the tawny shape of a fully grown lion, asleep on the sand.

This is another very lucky encounter, and slowly and quietly we approach. The wind is in our favour. We inch forward, under a large river acacia, and get within twenty yards of the animal. He is still asleep. We stop and watch his great chest rise and lower, and we can see flies circling and landing. Iain is sniffing the air and whispers, 'I think I can smell a kill. Either that, or somebody is letting go some very nasty farts.'

Then the lion senses us. Has the wind shifted, or did he hear us whispering, or did a bird chirp differently? He raises up, looks at us, and for two seconds we have eye contact. His body is covered by hair so short he almost looks hairless. He is a large male, and like all mature male lions in Tsavo, he has no mane, only a crest of a hair about an inch long, and longer stubbles on his jowls. Then he jumps up and runs into the bush.

We walk over to his bed and Danny reaches down and feels the sand. 'Happy full lion,' he says. Mohamed follows the animal's tracks and a moment later calls to us. We walk over and see the tall Samburu standing over the carcass of a buffalo. It is gutted and the hindquarters have been eaten, but there is still a substantial amount of meat left. Fifty feet away we discover the guts buried in the sand, and Danny says this is common. There is a deep groove from here to the carcass, suggesting this burial site of the guts is also where the buffalo was killed.

'It was probably more than the one lion that got it,' Bongo says. 'It's very violent, a kill of a big buffalo. Not a pretty sight.'

Of the big cats, lions are the most improvisatorial hunters. George Schaller, the well-known field researcher, studied lions in the Serengeti Plain for three years and counted eight different ways that lions hunt. The most effective is communal hunting, and this is almost always used in taking a big animal such as buffalo. Lions will usually grab the animal with their powerful forepaws, and as one tries to pull it down others go for its throat, to strangle it, or for its mouth, to suffocate it. In Tsavo, however, lions never form large prides as they do in the Serengeti, and when they do hunt together, they usually do it in pairs, which makes the kill of this buffalo even more impressive.

Individual lions (or pairs) will often acquire a favourite method of hunting, and of the various techniques they adopt perhaps the most fascinating to observe is the stalk. A lion is not a fast runner, and it must use every available cover to approach a prey. A stalk can take a half hour or more, but when the moment of the kill comes, it is, as Schaller described it, 'a drama in which it [is] impossible not to participate emotionally, knowing that the death of a being [hangs] in the balance.'

RORY NUGENT

# DRUMS ALONG THE CONGO
## On the Trail of Mokele-Mbembe, the Last Living Dinosaur

T HE WITCH DOCTOR curses. No one told him it was an American coming for the cure. His black eyes bore into mine, probing for something deep inside me. Bright-coloured plastic toothpicks pierce his earlobes, and a string of wooden fetishes bounce menacingly across his chest.

'Can you help?' Ambroise, my guide, challenges.

The witch doctor, Fortunado, winces and moves to the left, until our shadows no longer cross. He mumbles something inaudible and shakes his head.

'He has brought money,' Ambroise offers as I pull out a wad of West African francs.

The witch doctor surveys me again. After a moment he announces that I'm dirty and that my stink offends the gods, but if I'm willing to pay the price, he will cleanse me of evil. As I hold out the cash, he's careful not to touch my hand. He nods after counting the bills.

'*Déshabillez!*' the witch doctor barks.

Off come my shoes and socks, but not fast enough.

'*Vite! Vite!*' He doesn't have all day. People all over the Congo await him. He has potions to concoct and spells to cast.

Grabbing the front of my shirt, he repeats in French, 'To skin . . . to skin.' For good measure, he kicks my shoes across the courtyard.

'Hurry, you're pissing him off,' Ambroise hisses.

I've been in Brazzaville for over a month now, and I'm beginning to wonder if I'll ever be allowed beyond its limits. Congolese officials have been generous with their coffee and croissants, but not with their travel permits. My proposed destination, Lake Télé, fabled home of the supreme jungle deity, Mokele-Mbembe, is off-limits to foreigners without a special pass.

'Wear yourself naked,' the witch doctor insists and gestures feverishly at my underwear. Reluctant, I thumb the elastic waist-band, recalling how I arrived at this odd situation.

Yesterday, after a particularly long and unproductive meeting with government officials, Ambroise concluded that my approach was all wrong. I must first beseech Mokele-Mbembe and then petition the government for permission to visit Lake Télé.

'God before man,' Ambroise insisted. 'And to reach Mokele-Mbembe you must be cleansed . . . It's the only way.'

A small group of men has gathered in the courtyard. The witch doctor scowls as Ambroise urges, 'Do it . . . Come on, do it.'

I suppose a few minutes of public nudity here in the dust of the Bacongo district, miles from my hotel, won't damage my reputation any further.

'Now we will begin.' The witch doctor hurls my boxer shorts into the air.

He signals to Ambroise, and the two of them vanish into the witch doctor's house, leaving me stark naked to the gawking crowd. A *mundélé*, or white man, let alone his genitals, is a rare sight in this neighbourhood, and more and more men trickle into the courtyard fenced by a hodgepodge of mud bricks and stones.

I seek the shade and lean against a wall, trying to ignore the wide eyes staring at me. A mongrel trots over for a quick sniff and attempts to mount my leg. A kind gentleman calls the dog and boots it into the street.

Voices are coming from inside the house, but the words are muffled by drawn curtains imprinted with portraits of President Denis Sassou-Nguesso, the Maoist who rose to power in 1979. The talking continues, seconds tick by like hours, and my patience expires. I poke my head through the doorway, interrupting the clink of glasses. Ambroise and Fortunado are sitting comfortably at a table sipping whisky.

'A toast to a successful cleansing.' Ambroise hoists his glass.

*'Oui.'* The witch doctor tosses back his drink and quickly refills his tumbler.

I turn on my heels with a loud harumph and storm back to the courtyard. The curious onlookers retreat to a safe distance as one agitated stranger scrambles for his clothes. The witch doctor bursts from the house and snatches the shirt from my hand. He waves a Fanta bottle filled with a thick, golden liquid.

*'Regardez!'* He jiggles the bottle.

Intrigued, I watch as he holds it up to the sun. Scores of insects are suspended in the amber goo, and he seems to be clicking his tongue at each one. He plucks a toothpick from his earlobe and jabs it into the neck of the bottle. Then a curious silence ensues. I wonder if the insects convey some cosmic meaning, a horoscope perhaps.

'Are the signs good?' I ask, eager to learn my lot.

'Silence!'

I have had Hindus predict the future from my shadow, and Tibetan lamas have divined my fate from blades of grass tossed in the air, but this oracle of insects is new to me. Most soothsayers in this area rely on a divining board sprinkled with sand; the believer shakes the board, and the resulting lines are interpreted by an Ife-trained fortune-teller. I look for Ambroise, who is moving through the crowd, proudly telling people that he's the one who has brought the *mundélé*.

'Ambroise! What does the witch doctor see?'

Ambroise questions the priest in Lingala, an ancient Bantu language that has a soft, musical quality, with repetitive vowel sounds and drawn-out *f*s.

'He sees many colours.'

'What?'

He shrugs. 'That's what he said . . . many pretty colours.'

At last the witch doctor puts down the Fanta bottle and surrounds it with small rocks and dirt. He returns the toothpick to his left ear and removes his rings and bracelets. He motions me into the middle of the courtyard, exposing me to an unblinking equatorial sun. Almost immediately sweat begins to flow down my body, and I wonder how long it will be until my pink skin scalds. The sun's withering stare, Ambroise says, is essential to the cleansing process.

The witch doctor rises on the balls of his feet, stretches his arms skyward, and begins opening and closing his hands rhythmically. His eyes shut tight, he gulps mouthfuls of air to capture energy from the sky gods. Invigorated, he stomps toward me and exhales an unearthly, high-pitched scream.

'Ambroise,' I plead from a puddle of sweat.

'Hush!'

The witch doctor spins like a dervish, whooping as he revolves. His necklace of fetishes dances to life, eerily animate. He raises one hand, bows, and, without warning, thrusts his contorted face into mine. Spittle sprays across my brow as he howls a painful sound. The crowd gasps in admiration. The witch doctor then tugs on his necklace and issues a spine-tingling trill for each fetish; I wonder if these vocal gymnastics are for the audience or the gods.

Suddenly the witch doctor becomes sombre and assumes a look of intense concentration. He appears to fall into a trance: his eyes glaze, saliva foams in the corners of his mouth, liquid runs from his nose, and his limbs twitch spasmodically.

'It's working,' Ambroise whispers. The people around him nod.

The sun is blazing hotter than ever, sapping my resolve. I can feel my bald pate frying, and a powerful thirst has seized me.

'Give me my hat.'

'No! . . . You must be naked.'

'I don't care. My hat, please!'

'Shhhh.'

The witch doctor, disturbed by our voices, emerges from his trance and wags a finger. Everything is going well; impatience, however, will sabotage the cleansing. He says he was communing with the gods and has their ear. Ambroise suggests I think about ice cubes.

A young boy fetches a galvanised bucket from the side of the house. A red liquid sloshes over the rim. The witch doctor mutters an incantation while dipping his fingertips into the bucket. He flicks the liquid at me, splattering my body with crimson dots.

'Doorways for the evil spirits,' Ambroise advises.

'Protect yourselves,' someone in the crowd warns. Instantly the onlookers start praying, aware that the ousted devils will soon be seeking new homes.

The witch doctor steps back to examine his work and adds a few more dots around my feet and navel. Apparently satisfied, he invokes a new sequence of chants, this time kissing a fetish at the start of each one. I feel myself growing faint as the sweat continues to roll off me. My head and shoulders are the colour of boiled lobsters. I groan when Fortunado instructs me to flap my arms like a bird.

'Inhale . . . exhale . . . inhale . . .' he orders.

'Drink the air he has purified. Force the devils out!' Ambroise coaches.

The witch doctor bows toward the sun and claps his hands twice. The crowd cheers as he turns and slaps the tender skin on my back.

'Success!' Ambroise trumpets. 'You are clean . . . no more devils.'

I thank the witch doctor and scurry for the shade. He chases after me and yanks me back into the sunlight. The ceremony is not over.

'Hold on. He must seal you from the new devils trying to get back in.'

'What?'

'Silence!' The witch doctor picks up the solar-heated Fanta bottle and positions it directly over my head. With a blurp, the sacred potion plops on to my head, much to the amusement of the crowd. Slowly he spreads the jellied substance over my entire body, methodically working his way down to my toes.

The potion has a noxious odour that stings my nostrils. The stench alone should keep devils away. The crowd swings upwind, pinching their noses and dousing their handkerchiefs with perfume.

'I can hardly breathe!' I gag and shut my eyes, irritated by the goo.

'The potion is very powerful,' Ambroise observes.

'What's in it?' A bittersweet taste creeps into my mouth. I can hear Ambroise talking to Fortunado as the liquid oozes between my buttocks.

'He says there are many ingredients. Some are secrets, but he did say crocodile oil and honey and bits of . . .'

I feel a tickling all over and, opening my eyes, I see that I'm shrouded with insects; flies dine on my torso; honeybees graze on my shoulders; tiny beetles crawl in my pubic hair; millipedes picnic in the shade of my insteps; a queue of black ants is working its way up my right leg. As I move to brush them off, the witch doctor pins my arms.

'Be strong,' he says, his hands circling my wrists.

'Stand still,' Ambroise adds, 'and show the devils how strong you are.'

The itching is unbearable. Every winged insect within a half kilometre has picked up the scent and swarmed to this six-foot-two-inch lollipop. I recall reading that the Bateke tribes upriver used a similar method to punish infidelity. An adulterer would be slathered with honey, bound to a tree deep in the rainforest, and left to be eaten piecemeal; supposedly the practice stopped decades ago.

'You should see yourself, *très formidable*,' Ambroise pipes gleefully.

Cloaked with insects, I shimmer in the sunlight, a mosaic of iridescent wings, amethyst bodies, emerald fur, cobalt shells, yellow shields and glistening eyes. The odour of the rancid potion knots my stomach. In the dust I spot a column of driver ants wending its way toward me; wasps start nibbling in the right crease of my crotch, arching their backs and exposing their stingers in a harvest dance.

'Please, O Holy One,' I whine.

He finally releases his grip, saying that it's important for all the insects to return to the gods fat and happy. 'You are free of devils . . . Now go to the river and wash.'

'Follow him.' Ambroise points to a boy running out of the courtyard.

Snatching up my cap and underwear, I streak off, shedding bugs with every step. The young boy leads me down an unpaved street that dead-ends at the Congo River. He jumps from boulder to boulder and finally points out a rock pool close to the river's edge. He hands me a bar of soap and takes a seat. The crowd from the cleansing has followed and applauds the witch doctor as he arrives. Fishermen leave their traps to see what the commotion is all about. The goo does not scrub off easily; I have to scour my already raw skin with mud and sand before the soap does any good. Ambroise stands on the riverbank telling anyone who will listen that he's my redeemer.

'It took weeks to convince the *mundélé* . . . My prayers worked . . . Yes, I arranged everything.'

As I head to the main stream to rinse off, the boy jumps up and grabs my arm. The deep water isn't safe, he signals. He points beyond the fishing traps to a line of turbulence that marks the beginning of the rapids and tosses a stick into the river. We watch it spin convulsively downstream, caught in a deceptively swift current. I submerge in the shallows.

'I hope you see Mokele-Mbembe,' the witch doctor shouts from the bank, turning to leave.

'Here are your clothes. I'll be at Fortunado's when you finish.' Ambroise jogs to catch up with the priest. They walk arm in arm down the street and out of sight, followed by the crowd and the young boy. The fishermen finish their cigarettes and go back to work.

Alone, I float on my back and close my eyes. An image of the god-beast Mokele-Mbembe gradually comes to me. The long, thin-necked sauropod is holding court on the lush shores of Lake Télé. All sorts of jungle creatures are in attendance: duikers, bongos, reedbucks, sitangs, okapis, jungle cats, galagos, chimps and gorillas pay homage. Monkeys adorn the god with liana necklaces strung with orchids and periwinkle; orioles, sunbirds, hawk eagles, coucals, swifts, trogons and parrots deposit fruit at its feet. The god-beast looks at me and nods its gigantic head, as if to say, 'Sure, come visit . . . we'll be expecting you.'

The next morning Ambroise and I meet outside his office building, a four-storey cement blockhouse designed by Romanians, engineered by Chinese and paid for by Soviets.

'You must be feeling great,' Ambroise gushes as we stride toward the Ministry of Forests. 'And you look so clean . . . Now you will surely get the permit.'

However, I'm not issued a permit that day or even that month; in fact, my situation begins to deteriorate. The officials start asking me to pay for the coffee and croissants.

'Hmmm. Some devils must have returned. We should visit Fortunado again,' Ambroise suggests, but I keep walking in the shade.

KEVIN KERTSCHER

# AFRICA SOLO
## A Journey across the Sahara, Sahel, and Congo

I SET OUT FROM GOMA to see the mountain gorillas on Good Friday. It was raining again when I left town. The rainy season had definitely arrived and I could only imagine what the muddy roads I had travelled the previous weeks looked like now. Heading back north and then east towards the border, there were numerous steep volcanic hills, many of them rising right up out of the flat farmland like jagged teeth. Everything was either dark green or dark brown, the rich volcanic soil showing through even in the places where the crops were full grown. The gorilla reserve was in the biggest of the mountains up in the Virunga National Park, tucked in a border zone where Zaire, Rwanda and Uganda all come together.

I was dropped off in a village near the main road and spent a few hours hiking on a gradual incline, just to get to the base of the mountain. Then I began a long hike up to the lodge. The views on the way up were terrific, but it was much farther than I had expected. When I finally saw the lodge appear, I was so grateful that I laid down in the grass to let the sweat dry a bit before making the final assault. My clothes were already wet from the rain, and with the humidity, nothing was drying quickly.

When I got up to start walking again, a man was coming down from the lodge to meet me. He was blond and Caucasian, and he gave a big wave when he saw me standing. I couldn't imagine what he might want and we both walked another ten minutes before finally reaching each other. He welcomed me and deferentially introduced himself as the manager of the lodge. He wanted to carry my backpack, but I wouldn't let him, so he took my day pack instead. We made small talk as we trudged up the hill and were nearly to the beautiful glass and wood lodge, perched right on the ridge, when we realised that he had mistaken me for a different customer. His demeanour quickly changed.

'I'm terribly sorry, you're not in our lodge at all,' he said, somewhat annoyed. 'You would be in the cabin over there.' He pointed to a big, rustic log cabin that was another two-thirds of a mile up the ridgeline.

'Well, thanks for carrying the bag,' I said to him while eye-balling the white-coated, white-gloved African attendants who were staring at me.

'How much is your place anyway?' I asked, thinking his lodge looked so nice that I might splurge for a fifteen- or twenty-dollar room. He gave me a price list that showed rooms starting at $375, meals included. The lodge was owned and run by the famous safari resort TreeTops, and the brochure indicated it had been open just three months.

'Thanks, I'll give it some thought,' I said, pulling my pack back on and heading off to the cabin. I passed the rangers' station, the small visitors' centre, and after fifteen minutes got to the big log cabin. It was a classic park cabin with a central kitchen and a bunk room on each side, one for men and one for women. I was the only one there. Signs said that it was built and maintained by the Frankfurt Zoological Society. There was firewood stashed neatly next to the stove, jugs of fresh water, and utensils for cooking and eating. The front porch looked out onto the valley that I had come from, grey clouds, green volcanic mountains, checkerboard farm fields all down below. And it was quiet – so quiet that I didn't quite know what to do with myself. I could feel the temperature dropping, so I got a fire going in the stove and changed into dry, warm clothes and then sat out on the porch for an hour and a half thinking and watching the sun set. It felt almost tragic to be there all alone, and at the same time I felt like the luckiest person in the world.

I listened for gorilla noises, but I didn't hear any, even though the thick forest started just behind the cabin. I could see a good bit of their habitat because there was a high peak nearby that marked the place where the three borders met, with acres and acres of trees leading all the way up to it. In various patches of that forest, I knew that there were families of gorillas moving through the trees, eating, mating, fighting, bedding down for the night. As I sat on the porch, watching the stars and listening to the night, I remembered my great-great-uncle who had spent months exploring and tracking gorillas in the same region seventy years ago. He had gone home with journals full of scientific observations, hundreds of animal skins, and three small mountain gorillas – the first ever brought to Europe and America in captivity. I wondered what he had thought when he camped in these mountains. Had he seen the same skies outside his safari tent? Had he heard the same noises in the night? Had he felt the same nervous excitement?

At 6.30 in the morning, after lying awake much of the night, I got up to stoke the fire and watch the sun rise. It had gotten very cold during the night and I quickly boiled some water to make a hot cup of tea. At 7.15, I saw a few of the rangers gathering at the station and I went down to talk to them. I had been given some materials that explained the gorilla visits, but it had been so quiet on the hilltop that I wasn't even sure we'd be going.

From far away these Zairian men looked sharply dressed in their khaki uniforms, but up close, they were a scraggly bunch. They told me that there were only two other tourists at the TreeTops lodge, and that if those tourists chose to take an afternoon visit, I would be going alone with the rangers in the morning. It was the beginning of the off-season, they told me, and they were scheduled to stop the tours for a three-month break in another week and a half.

I went back to the cabin and had a piece of bread and more tea for breakfast, got dressed for the day, and then went to the small visitors' centre to look at some of the pictures until it was time to go. There was a history of the gorilla visits and some information on how to interact with them. The gorillas moved in families of about thirty to forty, it said, with one silverback as the leader, ten to twenty 'mamas', and usually ten to fifteen youngsters at one time. When the male children got old enough, they would go off on their own until they were strong enough to challenge another silverback for the control of a family. The traditional image of the mountain gorilla beating its chest was primarily a product of those male to male encounters, the exhibit said, but it was also a part of the gorilla's whole system of avoiding conflict through intimidation.

The gorillas that lived in the mountains nearby had been slowly habituated to the presence of humans. They now tolerated humans as they would other animals in the forest, but if we got inside their space, the females would react first by growling and charging. If the silverback thought that there was any real threat to his group, then the consequences could be more serious. He would first show his anger with thunderous roars and chest pounding, then warning charges, and finally real fighting charges. Most of the females were about four-and-a-half feet tall and weighed nearly six hundred pounds, the literature said, while the silverbacks were typically about a foot taller and weighed over one thousand pounds, with chests even wider around than they were tall. If one charged, the park commission advised, you should tuck up in a ball and let them bat you around a few times. If you didn't run or fight back, they would almost never harm you.

When I went outside, the guards, who were armed with rifles and machetes, reiterated the last part. 'If they charge, just cover your head and stay still,' they said. I was disappointed to see that the couple from the lodge had decided to come along. They were in their fifties and looked like they had just stepped out of an Abercrombie and Fitch catalogue. They were so clean and well-pressed that at first I had trouble concentrating on what they were saying. I hadn't seen anyone who looked so well-groomed since I'd left Europe. I wondered what they thought of me, with my worn jeans, my well-weathered blue T-shirt and the windbreaker that I'd been laundering in muddy water for three months. They seemed a little disappointed that I was there, but mostly they were just nervous about the gorillas, especially the woman, who almost lost her nerve after the rangers went through the warnings.

At about 8.30, we all hiked into the forest on a path that started right behind my cabin. There were three of the local rangers with us, two in front and one in back. The lead guide was the tracker. It was his job to find where one of the nearby gorilla families had slept the night before, and then follow their tracks to where they were feeding that morning. In this way, the rangers charted the movements and made a head count of three or four different families each day. By coordinating with similar programs in Rwanda and Uganda, and by moving quickly against poachers over the past seven years, they had stabilised the rapidly declining gorilla population in that preserve at about 200 – half of the wild population in the world. There were some indications that the population was starting to increase again, though inbreeding had become almost as big a problem as poaching.

We walked quietly through the thick woods for over an hour before we found nests from the night before. Each was a pile of recently broken branches and leaves with a round depression from their weight and a small brown piece of gorilla spoor in the middle. In the thick forest, the gorillas had stripped enough leaves off the plants around their sleeping area that some sunlight was allowed to get in. As we stood there illuminated by shafts of light, my heart started beating faster knowing that the large animals had been there just a few hours before and that they were undoubtedly nearby. The wealthy couple stood almost back to back, their eyes wide as they searched the forest in every direction.

The head guide picked a piece of the gorilla dung out of one of the larger nests, squeezed it a little and then held it up under his nose. He studied nearby branches, checking to see how they were broken, and then motioned for us to follow deeper into the forest. 'Same, every day,' one of the rangers whispered to me as he pointed to the nests, meaning that the gorillas would defecate in their nests before heading out for the day. 'Warm is nearby,' he said. 'Cold is not near.'

'Why does he smell it?' I asked. The ranger thought about this and shrugged.

Every few hundred yards we would stop and listen for a moment, and the tracker would inspect the ground and the trees for signs. He was so theatrical about it that I started to think he was just kidding around. But one time when we stopped he held his hand up for us to be quiet and we could hear some branches breaking nearby. I didn't see anything initially, but when I looked toward one of the noises, I could see a big patch of black in with the green, then another and another. We took a few steps forward and soon branches were crackling all around us. There were gorillas everywhere, even little ones in the trees above.

My impulse was to back right out of there, but the gorillas' countenance was so gentle that they soon put me at ease. When we moved slowly around to get a better look at some of them, they just watched us shyly and continued eating their leaves. The big silverback looked twice the size of the others. He stayed a short distance apart, wreaking havoc on a big patch of stalks, eating as much as he could lazily fit in his mouth. He ignored us for the most part, keeping his back to us and grunting occasionally if we moved near his space.

In his pack, he had twenty-three 'mamas', seven babies, and a few young males who were already starting to show a little silver, but were not yet big enough to be kicked out of the clan. The biggest of the babies ran up and down the trees and stalks, wrestling with each other and annoying the older gorillas. Two of them climbed out on some of the high stalks, going farther and farther until the stalks broke, dropping them right on top of some of the feeding mothers. They were sent tumbling with a quick swat and a growl, and then they went looking for some other stalks and did it again.

The smallest babies were more sedate, little fur balls just learning to crawl and climb. The littlest one became curious about us and crawled right over to me to take a closer look. I squatted down with my arms resting on my knees and he reached out to touch my forearm, running his little leathery finger back and forth

41

on my bare skin. He was so irresistibly cute that I wanted to pick him up. But the mama who appeared to be the babysitter started growling and one of the rangers asked me to move aside as he carefully pushed the baby away with the butt of his rifle. This made the mama more angry and she charged right at me, moving like lightning and baring her sharp teeth. I took a step back and ducked my head. But she had pulled up a few feet away and saun- tered off into the jungle, following the silverback who had decided to move to another spot. I was a little embarrassed that I had jumped back when the rangers had been so emphatic about not running from the gorillas, but when I looked up, the guard who had been next to me was five feet back and the rest of the party was ten feet behind him.

We stayed with them for an hour, following them each time they moved to a new feeding site. The guards said that they thought the baby had touched me because I was wearing a short- sleeve shirt and he had never seen such white skin. I put my jacket on and we tried to stay a little further back, but the same mother charged me again, this time swiping her hand so close to my head that I felt my hair move. I was squatting down this time and I just turned my head and shoulders away. By the time I glanced up, she was already twenty feet away.

But by then I found I wasn't really frightened. They were so obviously gentle and so aware of their surroundings that I felt totally trusting of them. 'No one who looks into a gorilla's eyes – intelligent, gentle, vulnerable – can remain unchanged . . .' the naturalist George Schaller once wrote, and I understood what he meant. They looked like they might start speaking if you stayed long enough. But I could also tell that after a while we were being intrusive and bothersome by constantly following them. Finally the silverback went into an area of thick brush where we couldn't follow, and he growled a few times as if to say, 'Okay, the ses- sion's over. Get out of here.' A few of the mamas had to cross by us to follow him, and the babysitter who had feint-charged twice decided to just sit on the path in front of us. We waited for a little while, but then she sat back defiantly and started eating a nearby shrub. The head guide decided to scare her away by dropping a thin tree near her. It was a good plan except that the tree was taller than he thought and the branches fell right on top of her. This time when she charged she really was mad, but she still didn't do anything except scare the heck out of the ranger.

We left reluctantly, looking back often as we walked in silence through the depths of green leaves and yellow light. When we stepped back out of the forest, it was like stepping out of a dream.

# OCEANIA

TONY HORWITZ

# ONE FOR THE ROAD
Hitchhiking through the Australian
Outback

**T**HERE'S ONLY one thing I dread more than setting up camp at night in the Great Outdoors, and that's breaking camp at morning in the Great Outdoors. At least in the dark you can just curl up in your bag and be done with it – if there are no cyclones lurking about. But mornings are pure hell. I like to wake slowly, over a cup of coffee and the sports page, not scramble around in the dawn chill for socks and shoes, then hike off for a 'dingo's breakfast' – a pee and a good look around. That's my idea of a lousy way to start the day.

Weathering a hurricane has one advantage. Since I've got my entire wardrobe on already, all I have to do is shed a few layers into my pack and hike out to the road. The night breeze has died down, from cyclone to mere gale-force winds, so I'm reasonably cosy, propped against my pack with a blanket around my shoulders.

If I only had some food. It is part of my poor camping technique to never have victuals on hand when I'm a million miles from nowhere. And there's still no sign of a proprietor at the roadhouse. Maybe he's asleep, as any sensible person would be at this hour. Maybe I should wake him up. Maybe he's awake already, cooking me two dozen flapjacks with six fried eggs smiling on top, and coffee strong enough to kick-start a cadaver. Then again, maybe he's off shopping in Alice.

I try to distract myself by reciting 'The Love Song of J. Alfred Prufrock'. I memorised the first few stanzas between Sydney and Alice, but now, in the middle of the poem, I keep getting stuck on the same two lines: 'I have measured out my life in coffee spoons' and 'Would it have been worth it, after all, after the cups, the marmalade, the tea'. The whole poem's about breakfast if you read it right.

My imaginary marmalade and tea is interrupted by a very unpoetic roar down the road. bbbbbbrrrrrr. BBBBBrrrrrrrr! I squint at the horizon. It looks as if the night wind has blown away all the trees, hills and scrub. The landscape is so flat and bare that I feel as if I might be able to see all the way to Alice. But all I can pick out is a tiny speck, coming toward me, going bbbbrrrrr, BBBBBrrrrrr! It is moving at a pained, slow crawl, like me before my morning coffee. A few minutes later, the ute limps to a halt beside me. There are four Aboriginal men staring sullenly out from the cab and a dozen jerry cans of petrol vibrating in the back. Judging from the noise, there's some kind of prehistoric beast with pins stuck in its nose stuffed under the bonnet.

'Where ya headed?' I shout at the driver, a very black man with a massive bush of hair. He looks at me blankly. I point at the southern horizon and bob my head up and down.

'Pedy,' he mumbles. I point at the back of the truck, then at myself and bob my head again.

'Hey, mate. OK,' he mumbles. I scramble into the back and squeeze myself between two petrol drums, like a stowaway on an oil tanker. We rumble off at twelve miles an hour and the hideous noise starts again. BBBRRRRRRRRRRRR! I have gone from the eye of a hurricane to the belly of a sick, screaming whale. BBBBBBBBRRRRRRRRRRRRRR! I toss the blanket over my head again and the noise goes down a decibel or two. BBBbbbbbrrrrrrrr. It's beginning to look like another underwear job.

It's also beginning to look like a very slow drive to Coober Pedy. Ten minutes down the road, the driver stops and feeds the monster a drum of petrol. Then he rolls the empty barrel into the scrub and hops in beside me, letting someone else take the wheel. I offer the three words of Pitjantjatjara I picked up at Ayers Rock–Uluru: *paya* (thank you) and *rama-rama* (crazy). He offers his sum total of English – OK, hey, mate, yes. We shout our three words in every possible combination, then smile and nod at each other for 125 miles.

Actually, it's hard not to nod when you're swerving and bumping over a road that's like gravel laid over choppy surf. Only the oil drums keep me from going overboard. And there's nothing to look at except a cloud of dust shooting out behind the truck, with glimpses to either side of baked and empty desert. By mid-morning, the heat becomes staggering; even in the windblown rear of the ute, I can feel the sun burning every inch of exposed flesh. Nothing to do but huddle beneath my blanket, wedge some of it under my bum as a shock absorber, and tough it out.

A few hours later my companion squeezes up front again with his mates. Then something strange happens. The ute veers off the main road (such as it is) and on to what looks like a dingo trail. I clutch the side of the truck as we bounce between bushes and churn through deep sand. I have a hitchhiker's distrust of detours, particularly when the main road is itself a detour from any habitable territory.

I bang on the back window and get no response; apparently, there's some kind of domestic squabble going on up front. The ute lurches to a halt behind a clump of mulga and the four men pile out, talking loudly in Pitjantjatjara and gesturing at me. All I know is that something ugly is about to happen, and whatever it is, I'm along for the ride.

One thing's for sure; I'm not going to talk my way out of this one, whatever it is. All I can do is listen to their chatter and let my paranoia run riot in translation. ('How much money do you think he has?' 'Do we kill him or just leave him here to bake?') Nor can I sort of mosey of into the scrub – 'Some other time, fellas' – and run for it. Not here, at the centre of the bottomless dustbowl that is outback South Australia. I'd make it three hours at the most before collapsing of heat exhaustion, dehydration, or worse.

'Hey, mate!' It is the driver speaking. He is walking toward me, sweating nervously, with one hand clutching something in his pocket.

'Hey, mate!' He pulls his hand out and thrusts it toward me. I freeze. Then his fist uncurls to reveal a pile of crumpled two-dollar notes.

'OK, yes!' he shouts.

I look at him blankly. Yes, what? He's exhausted his English and his body language isn't helping. Nor does my extensive Pitjantjatjara vocabulary seem appropriate. Rama-rama? Uluru?

'Grog, mate,' says one of his companions. 'Black fellas can't buy us grog.'

We move to dust language now and he draws a map headed back the way we came. South of the spot where we turned off, he sketches a square, and what looks like a bottle. 'Black fellas can't buy us grog,' he repeats, handing me the money and the key to the ute. 'Two, mate.'

Slowly I get the picture. They want me to take their money, and their truck, and drive to the roadhouse to buy two cases of beer. For some reason – a racist publican, I assume – they can't buy it themselves. They'll wait here until I return.

The request says a lot about their trust and my lack of it. All I have done to win their confidence is utter three words of pidgin Pitjantjatjara. All they have done to lose my trust is talk loudly in a language I don't understand. Paranoia took care of the rest.

My first reaction is relief that nothing sinister is afoot and that I can atone for my suspicions by helping them out. For the first time on my journey, I feel as if I've violated the unwritten contract of trust between hitchhiker and hitchhikee. But they don't know that, and anyway, I can make up for it by buying a few beers.

But as I dodge sand traps on my way back to the main road, another dilemma surfaces. I am not by nature an interventionist on the matter of personal habit. Live and let live; drink and let them get drunk. That's the reckless half of my hitchhiker's valour. The discreet hitchhiker in me is screaming caution. We are still 200 miles of rough empty road from Coober Pedy. With a case or two of beer on board, it could be a long, even futile journey.

Or is this prejudice again, welling up in the background as it threatened to do a moment ago, when I began hearing the racist chorus of Territory voices I've managed to ignore until now? . . . 'Don't turn your back on a black fella . . .' 'An Abo will cut your throat faster than you can say boomerang . . .' 'Whatever you do, mate, don't take a ride with boongs.'

My contact with Aborigines has consistently contradicted these dire warnings. From Cunnamulla to Tennant Creek to Ayers Rock, I've been treated by blacks with an openness and generosity not always evident among whites. This last incident is further proof of Aboriginal goodwill. How many white drivers would entrust a scruffy hitchhiker with their piggy bank and sole means of transportation?

That's what makes me nervous; there is a whiff of desperation about the request. But the real problem is, I have no way of knowing if this will lead to a blow-out, and no way of coping if it does. North of Alice, there was the occasional roadhouse at which to abandon ship. Here, nothing; we haven't even seen another car in four hours. The barrier between us isn't racial, it's linguistic. If things get sloppy, which they easily can after two cases of beer, we'll need more than dust drawings to sort the situation out.

As the roadhouse comes into view, I am leaning toward a compromise. My instinct is confirmed by a huge sign above the bar, which announces that it's illegal to buy alcohol before heading into Aboriginal territory. Two cases of beer might make me conspicuous. Two six-packs won't, and it also won't be enough to leave me on a walkabout in the South Australian desert.

The publican is the only person in the pub and he doesn't ask any questions. So I load up the beer, and fill my tucker box with stale bread and overpriced cheese. Then, just for security, I order a meat pie as well. After hours with no food, the microwaved chunks of meat go down like *coq au vin*. Picky eaters don't survive a day of roadhouse cuisine.

My companions appear unsurprised when I return with most of their money unspent and only a dozen beers. And the speed with which the tinnies are drained, crushed and tossed into the scrub quiets any qualms I had about disobeying orders.

I am about to pass around my bread and cheese when two of the men begin helping themselves. Their offhand manner makes me realise that the gesture is neither rude nor ravenous. Rather, it seems that food and drink are assumed to be public domain. Every twenty minutes or so through the morning, a waterbag and a lit cigarette were passed to me in the back of the truck. This was my ration, my right as an occupant of the ute. It would be inappropriate – even insulting – to suggest that my food was anything but part of the collective. We eat a few slices each, share the waterbag and cigarette pack, and climb aboard for the long drive to Coober Pedy.

This time my companion in the back is Joe, he of the 'black fellas can't buy us grog'. His English is good enough for a halting dialogue interspersed with sign language and sketches on the dusty side of an oil drum. As far as I can make out, the men are travelling from their home on a reserve in the Northern Territory to spend a few weeks 'noodling' for opal around Coober Pedy. Noodling, as Joe describes it, is a leisurely sort of look-see through the piles of rubble left by white miners and white machines.

'White fellas always go, go go,' Joe says, pantomiming men driving drills and pickaxes into the ground. 'They miss so much riches that way.' Noodling, it seems, is not a bad metaphor for the difference between our cultures.

Indeed, Joe doesn't miss a beat along the sixty miles of unsealed road we travel after stopping for beer. Every ten minutes or so he touches me on the arm and points off toward an empty horizon. Each time there is an emu or kangaroo, almost invisible to me, but obvious as a skyscraper to Joe. The foreground is clear enough, though; long lines of abandoned automobiles stretching beside both sides of the road, like parallel queues to a scrapyard just over the horizon. Burnt cars, stripped cars, overturned cars. The place looks like a training camp for terrorist car bombers.

'Black fellas bad with cars,' Joe explains. 'No buy fixing out here.' At least there are plenty of dead cows to keep the car bodies company. But otherwise, nothing. It is as bare and bleak a landscape as I've ever clapped eyes on.

For several thousand miles, I've been struggling for un-superlatives to communicate the un-ness of outback scenery. The towns and people are easy enough; they have faces, buildings, features. But what can you say about a landscape that is utterly featureless? A landscape whose most distinguishing quality is that it has no distinguishing qualities whatsoever? Flat, bare, dry. Bleak, empty, arid. Barren, wretched, bleached. You can reshuffle the adjectives but the total is still the sum of its parts. And the total is still zero. Zot. Nought. Ayers Rock has a lot of blank space to answer for.

To the early explorers, this arid region north of Adelaide was simply Australia's 'Ghastly Blank'. Charles Sturt set off into the desert east of here in 1844 to find the inland sea, and so sure was he of success that his party included two sailors and a boat (as well as eleven horses, two hundred sheep, thirty bullocks and four drays). 'I shall envy that man who shall first place the flag of our native country in the centre of our adopted land,' he declared. But after staggering for some months through the desert, Sturt reached neither sea nor centre – just the dry expanse of Lake Torrens. 'The desolate barrenness, the dreary monotony, the denuded aspect of this spot is beyond description,' he wrote in his journal, having described it rather well. Daniel Brock, a member of Sturt's party added, 'This scene is the Climax of Desolation . . . Miserable! Horrible!' Not long after, Sturt launched his boat on the Darling River and then retreated to Adelaide.

Looking out the back of the ute I am amazed that Sturt made it as far as he did. Desert to the right of me, desert to the left of me, a plume of car dust shooting down the middle, I claim this spot as the landing pad for the alien probe I imagined my first day in Australia. The alien probe that drops down, declares 'No life,' and heads back to outer space. The probe people could sniff around here for a few hundred miles in every direction and come to the same conclusion. No life. No bloody way.

Just the sort of place you'd never want to break down in; just the thought that comes to me as the engine coughs and goes silent, leaving the ute half on and half off the highway. It seems the moaning beast under the bonnet has finally been put out of its misery.

The four men pile out and take turns staring through the steam rising out from under the bonnet. They study the ute's Japanese repair manual, upside down. Then they begin staring vacantly off into space. It is the noodling school of car repair. We are about to join the long queue of automobile corpses. Looking out at the empty desert, I don't like our chances either.

I am an automotive moron, a clod when it comes to all things mechanical. But desperation makes for marvellous self-improvement. Studying the manual, and then the tangle of metal under the bonnet, it becomes obvious to me that we no longer possess a fanbelt, if indeed we ever did. Also, whatever water the radiator once held is now evaporating on the ground at the rate of about fifty quarts per second.

Joe fashions a fanbelt by knotting the spare rubber flapping around under the bonnet. But feeding our meagre supply of water to the radiator seems a little risky. If we do, and the ute still doesn't move, we'll be fashioning straws to drink from the radiator within a few hours.

So once again I am called into service for the purpose of liquids procurement. While the four men huddle out of sight – or as out of sight as you can get in a desert, which means behind the ute – I wait for a passing car to beg some water from. It seems that for black fellas in this stretch of outback, water is as difficult to come by as beer.

The first car to pass is driven by a Romanian refugee named Milos. He's headed north from Adelaide to 'see some bush' and is happy to give me his entire water supply, all two quarts of it. I explain to him that there's no Danube running through South Australia and hand him his water back, along with the tourist guide the New Zealander gave me yesterday.

A short while later, two Aborigines pull up in a battered truck. When my companions hear the familiar, accented English of fellow blacks, they pop out from behind the ute like guests at a surprise party. The six men chat away for half an hour, then conversation is followed by a pirate raid on the newcomers' water, tucker and cigarettes. Then everyone begins chatting again. I assume that I'm witnessing a chance reunion of long-lost friends or relations. In actual fact, one of the newcomers tells me, they've met only once, on an earlier noodling expedition to Coober Pedy.

The colour of one's skin can be as powerful a bond in the outback as it can be a barrier.

An hour later, the party gets around to fixing the radiator. Water doesn't revive the ute. But with the truck pushing us from behind, the engine kicks into life again, or a tubercular version of it. We cough and wheeze down the highway for a hundred yards or so – before everyone decides this is cause for further celebration. So we pile out, chat and smoke for another half-hour, then get kick-started again down the road toward Coober Pedy.

Relieved, I let out an Indian war cry – *Yihaaaa! Yi-HAAAAAAAAAAAAA!* – and Joe imitates me for the hour-long drive. 'Do it one more,' he says, as if prompting a singer to repeat a favourite refrain. 'One more time, Tony.' The two of us are roughly the same colour from the waves of reddish-brown dust we've been swimming through all day. So there we sit, two red-skinned Apaches, belting out war cries all the way to the opal fields of South Australia.

Late in the day we reach Coober Pedy with the fanbelt still intact, the radiator cool. I climb out of the ute, shake each man's hand . . . 'Hey mate, OK' . . . 'Yes' . . . 'OK, yes' . . . and hoist my pack over one shoulder. It feels like a bag full of wet fish is crawling down my back. I yank the pack off and discover that one of the cans of diesel fuel has been leaking on to it for the past ten hours or so. The frame-and-canvas pack looks and feels like a soggy spring roll, abandoned in the grease for a few days. I think of all the lit cigarettes passed between Joe and the cab during the day, directly over the diesel-soaked pack. One stray ash and my clothes would have launched into outer space.

If they had, they might well have touched down in Coober Pedy. Lunar landscape is too generous a metaphor for this ugly, eerie place. Imagine, first of all, an endless plain of sand-coloured cones, spreading like an abandoned tent camp all the way to the horizon. That's the outskirts of town: a man-made – or man-ruined – expanse of dirt kicked up by the picks and bulldozers and explosives used to uncover opal.

The town itself is in perfect harmony with its surroundings, which is to say, as raw and ruined and forbidding a settlement as you'll find anywhere in the outback. It looks like an inhabited vacant lot. Abandoned and burnt-out cars litter the streets and yards like so much rusty lawn furniture. Discarded timber and sheets of corrugated iron are strewn about as well. And the dust is so thick when I arrive, several hours before sunset, that cars motor through slowly with their headlights on, as if piloting through fog.

Getting your bearings in Coober Pedy requires a kind of twisted sixth sense. There are few street signs and few real streets to speak of; just a dusty tangle of unpaved trails cutting every which way between the burnt-out cars and litter of timber and iron. Finding the inhabitants is almost as difficult. According to the tourist guide, there are 5,000 Coober Pedians, 'give or take a thousand'. Many of them are underground, if not in the mines, then in subterranean homes called 'dugouts'. All you can see from outside is a doorway set into the ridge, like the entrance to a mine shaft. That's home.

This molelike life-style began after World War I when miners rushed here to scratch for opal. Veterans mostly, fresh from the trenches of France, they got the bright idea of escaping the dust and blast-furnace temperatures by gouging underground. The habit survives today because it is cheaper to light a dugout than to air-condition an aboveground home through months of desert heat.

'This wing was started with pickaxes, then blown out with dynamite,' says Edward Radeka as nonchalantly as if he were showing off an addition to his split-level suburban home. In fact, he is leading me down a black tunnel to a room in Radeka's Underground Motel. 'Nice and quiet, don't you think?' The room is a cave, literally, with a bed and a chair beneath a canopy of shot-out stone. No windows, no natural light, just a few drawings hung from the stone and a small airshaft winding up to the earth's surface to let in a little oxygen. It looks like the kind of place where you could go to sleep and wake up in the next century.

Washing up isn't so easy. The name Coober Pedy is derived from an Aboriginal phrase meaning white man's burrow, or boy's waterhole, depending on which tourist brochure you look at. But whatever waterhole there once was has long since dried up. Now fluid comes in by truck or pipe and it costs about twenty dollars just to water the lawn. This explains why the only lawn in town belongs to the pub, which gets a helping hand from spilt beer. At the motel, Edward Radeka says I can have a bucketful of soapy water to wash with so long as I toss it on two of his stunted trees when I'm done.

The diesel fuel washes out well enough. But after an hour of drying on a Hills Hoist above the motel – that is, at ground level – my clothes are coated with a dense layer of reddish-brown dust. At least now they're colour-coordinated, with one another and with the colour of my skin.

At sunset I wander through town past underground homes, underground restaurants, underground bookshops. You can even pray underground in Coober Pedy at the Catacomb Church. About the only thing you can't do underground is find much opal, at least not any more. Apparently, the easy pickings are gone and most of the serious miners have moved off to Mintabie or other settlements. The only new work in the last few years came during the filming of *The Road Warrior*, when about 120 locals were hired to loll around as extras. They didn't really have to act, nor did the town require any modification; it is already a natural setting for a postnuclear fantasy.

After an hour of sightseeing – abandoned cars, humpies, broken glass – I stop to ask a man for directions to the nearest pub.

'You want to buy opal?' he answers in a strong Eastern European accent. I repeat my question and he repeats his. 'You want to buy opal?' I shake my head and he points me to a pub up the street. I have just had my first sip of beer at the bar when a man at the next stool edges over and whispers hoarsely in my ear: 'You want to buy opal?' Is this some kind of password or is every Coober Pedian a portable gem shop?

'Not many miners have a luck any more,' the man explains. 'But you can't sell small bits of opal so easy. So we make our tucker money by selling this way.'

Stief ('No last names, please. I not pay tax in nineteen years.') is a Yugoslav by birth, as are many of the miners in Coober Pedy. The town is so isolated that ethnic diferences have been preserved in a kind of Southern European aspic. Croatians gather at one end of the bar; Serbians at the other. And Italians and Greeks go to a different club altogether. 'Every nation in this place, except fair dinkum Aussies,' Stief says, wandering off to hustle another tourist at the bar. The phrase 'Want to buy opal?' is the Esperanto that joins all the different cultures together.

I leave in search of a souvlaki to fortify myself against the procession of pies and pasties on the road ahead. At nine o'clock the streets are almost silent. It seems that all the life has been coaxed out of Coober Pedy, along with the opal. Except for the gem sellers, of course. I am propositioned three times between the takeaway and the motel, twice by the 'Want to buy opal?' set and once by a tall, painted lady, whispering from the doorway of an opal shop.

'You have money I give you a sex.'

No, thank you, I have a sex. I have a souvlaki. All I want to do is get to my cave and go to sleep.

But there is one more voice in the night.

'Hey mate, OK!' It is Joe and company, greeting me from the ute, which is parked on the main street. Their eyes are glazed over with beer.

*'Rama-rama,'* I say, casting my arms around the town. Crazy.

Joe smiles. 'Say it one more time, Tony. One more time.' I shake my head, exhausted. So he does it for me, letting loose with a blood-curdling war cry into the desert air over Coober Pedy.

*'Yiiii-HAAAAAAAAAAAAAAAAAAAAAAA!'*

## ERIC HANSEN

# STRANGER IN THE FOREST
## On Foot across Borneo

A WARM, MOIST wind blew from the south down a valley lost in green folds of undulating rainforest. Carried on the wind were thick earthy smells of sweet-scented plants and decomposing leaf litter that carpeted the jungle floor. This enticing fragrance conveyed the first hints of what life would be like within the 120,000 square miles of rainforest that separated me from the coast by more than 400 miles.

Bo 'Hok, Weng and I left Pow-O-Pan before the sun had reached the valley floor. Roosters crowed intermittently, but few people were about as we shouldered our rattan packs and started towards the formidable-looking wall of big trees. Bo 'Hok and Weng walked ahead. We crossed a few hundred yards of garden plots, and then, as I watched, they nonchalantly stepped into the forest and disappeared from the world of settled village life. Moments later I, too, entered the forest. At first it seemed as if my guides had vanished, but then I caught sight of them. They moved silently, nearly obscured by the patterns of light and shade that rippled through the forest understorey. I hurried ahead to catch up with them. The sunlight soon dimmed and with it the last familiar traces of my own culture. Bo 'Hok and Weng were having quite the opposite experience. They disliked populated areas and direct sunlight, and it came as a relief to return to a familiar place where in the cool darkness no movement, sound or scent held a mystery. This jungle, so foreign to me, was their home; yet within minutes of entering it I felt myself willingly moving into a timeless world of natural rhythms.

The rainforest on this south-east side of the dividing range seemed drier and less slippery, but this may have been due to my improved balance and sure-footedness. The terrain was certainly flatter, but the most significant difference in the *feeling* of this portion of the jungle was its immense size. Whereas, when I left Long Seridan I knew I would be in the rainforest three or four weeks before arriving in a familiar place, I now had only a vague idea of where I was going and for how long. This uncertainty made me feel very vulnerable, but more important I had a very distinct physical reaction to the jungle. I could feel my body becoming tense and alert. I felt tight. The only similar sensation I can relate this to is the experience of swimming in the middle of the ocean where you *know* the water is many miles deep. The Kalimantan rainforest was like an uncharted, fathomless, green ocean, and I continued to nurture a healthy fear of the place.

We had entered a community of plants, insects and animals that has remained ecologically undisturbed for millions of years. The interwoven tangle of branches, lianas, ferns and orchids found in the Borneo rainforest sustains one of the world's most complex and least-studied ecosystems. The diversity of tree species alone is estimated at a staggering twenty-five hundred. In one ten-hectare sample plot of Borneo jungle, the Royal Geographical Society has identified nearly eight hundred species of trees. This is more than twenty times the total number of native tree species in all of Britain. This forest would be my home for the next eight weeks.

We moved through the damp jungle air, and the first sensation that returned to me was the mad, erratic, echoing cacophony of sounds, seemingly played by a group of quirky, invisible musicians. I'm referring to the insect hum, bird warble, animal cry, wind rush, tree-branch sigh and the incessant patter of water droplets on broad jungle leaves. In this twenty-four-hour, seven-day-a-week, primordial music hall a deranged orchestra played on laconically without need for a conductor or audience. At unexpected moments a succession of incongruent single notes would come to me from all sides, producing incomprehensible musical phrases. Discordant harmonies blared from high up in the jungle canopy only to be obliterated by staccato bursts of nearby insect sounds. The ground was alive with the rustling sounds, inaudible to the human ear, of millions of foraging insects (up to two thousand termites per square yard). The quietest activity of all came from the bacterial fungi, which steadily munch away at fallen leaves, gradually reducing them to perfect gauzelike skeletons.

I was spellbound by the dramatic interplay of shifting light and mysterious noises. One of the few bird sounds I could identify from the bewildering jumble of chitter-chatter, hoots and whistles was a babbler (genus *Malacoptera*) known as the Beethoven bird because it sings the familiar four opening notes of Beethoven's Fifth Symphony. Apart from this bird, and the by-now-familiar, frantic electronic buzzing of twenty species of cicadas, the origins of the sounds were a mystery to my untrained ear. There were literally hundreds of them, and I was to learn that each one held a special message for Bo 'Hok and Weng.

Perhaps it is too fanciful to compare the natural sounds of the jungle to structured music. In the rainforest there was certainly little to remind one of musical conventions, but the feelings evoked by these strange sounds had the same disturbing effects as music can have. I was hearing courtship calls, declarations of feeding territories, threats, warnings and startled shrieks of terror as unseen prey was torn to pieces by silent predators.

We were only a few hours' walk from Pow-O-Pan when we happened upon a living example of Kipling's giant red rock python from my childhood bedtime stories. The snake lay coiled on a river rock, iridescent and shimmering like a sinuous gem until Weng drew his parang and hacked the creature's head off during its midday nap. Weng fastened the writhing, headless, ten-foot-long snake to his pack, and we continued into the jungle – a place so bountiful and lush, yet so unforgiving of the slightest human weakness. We moved farther into this steaming, fetid world of great horrors and indescribable beauties whose elements were impossible to separate one from the other; and, as I learned, there was little sense in making simplistic distinctions of 'good' and 'bad'. As a visitor to the jungle, I was privileged to be allowed a brief glimpse of the natural patterns of plant and animal life on earth as they must have existed before the arrival of human beings. We were frail and insignificant creatures, and at any moment we could be swallowed up by the forest. When a plant, animal or human dies in the rainforest, it soon becomes a part of the forest. Flesh is digested, nutrients recycled, and body moisture reclaimed. The realisation that the rainforest was a living, breathing organism capable of consuming and digesting me was disconcerting, but also rather exciting. It made me feel as if we were travelling through the intestinal flora of some giant leafy creature.

Any fears that I may have entertained concerning my safety with Bo 'Hok and Weng were soon proved to be unjustified. Like Tingang Na and John Bong a month earlier, Bo 'Hok and Weng did their utmost to make me as comfortable as possible by anticipating my every need. Although they had had almost no contact with Westerners, they had a highly developed intuitive sense of what I was experiencing, and this gave me a strong sense of trust and safety. In Pow-O-Pan, Bo 'Hok and Weng had treated me with excessive formality. They had called me *Tuan*, which means 'Sir'; and, like *Bwana* in Swahili, the title carries the suggestion of 'white master', which made me feel uncomfortable. Fortunately, Bo 'Hok and Weng became more relaxed in the jungle. I always made a point of praising them on their extraordinary knowledge of the jungle, and soon the last traces of the white explorer–native guide relationship dissolved. This allowed me to start to develop our friendship. They called me Mister Eric and, less frequently, Rajah Kumis.

When we were sitting by the campfire the first night, I asked what they thought about the knife attack on Pilot Paul. From their expressions it was obvious that they were confused and troubled by the incident, and they admitted they did not know why people downriver did such things. We discussed acts of violence and crime beyond the jungle. Theft they could understand, but rape, mugging, suicide and murder were completely foreign to their way of living. Neither one of them could remember a Penan committing any of these acts.

'What would be a serious crime in the Penan community?' I asked.

They conversed for a minute, as though they were having difficulty thinking of any crime. Then Weng explained the concept of *see-bun*, which means to be stingy or not to share. An accusation of stinginess, I was told, could cause arguments and very bad feelings. Both Bo 'Hok and Weng expressed great surprise by clicking their tongues when I told them there were no laws in America regarding stinginess and that, in fact, stinginess or hoarding for oneself is esteemed and rewarded.

Social behaviour, from the Penan perspective, is judged in terms of what sorts of feelings result from different acts. Considering how close together these people live, it is not surprising that the feelings of others are of the greatest importance. As in traditional village law, certain offences in the jungle communities require compensation. Adultery was given as an example. 'Adultery,' Weng told me, 'can create bad feelings, and the offenders must pay a fine.' The payment for adultery varied, but it was never less than one cooking pot, a blowpipe and a parang. In special circumstances an additional payment of one good hunting dog and a spear might be required.

Whereas Tingang Na and John Bong, my two Penan guides in Sarawak, had settled with a few other families on the Magoh River to cultivate hill rice and tapioca, Bo 'Hok and Weng were still semi-nomadic. They spent three months of the year in a village cultivating crops, and the rest of the time they lived in the jungle and depended exclusively on forest resources. This more traditional lifestyle was reflected in their attitude towards the jungle. Their attitude was partially expressed in their manner of speech. For days their conversational style had me confused. They never spoke directly about anything, especially hunting. Also, they seemed extremely reluctant to refer to any kind of subsistence activity. Initially, I wondered if they were using a secret language to confuse me, but that was unlikely – if they had wanted to discuss something privately, they could have spoken Penan rather than Indonesian, our common second language.

Through observation and discussion I eventually discovered the purpose of their intentional vagueness. They frequently used the Penan expression *tie neet-neet*, which, roughly translated, means 'we're going to go to the jungle and pull our foreskins back'. I assumed this was a rather crude way of announcing they were going to have a pee. After these announcements, however, they would often take their shotguns and disappear for hours, returning later with game they had shot. *Tie neet-neet*, I discovered, actually indicated 'we're going hunting'. I questioned them further about their indirect manner of speaking, and they explained that it came from their great fear of forest spirits. Not necessarily a fear of personal harm, although that was a consideration, but fear that if the spirits were forewarned they would hide the game or food. Before hunting men will therefore not talk directly about guns, dogs or spears.

In certain circumstances both men and women use expressions that they consider to be disgusting or dirty. They do this hoping that the forest spirits will be equally disgusted and will keep away. One expression I frequently heard the Penan women in Sarawak use was explained to me by Weng. *Muee-loto*, the women would say. The expression means 'to go and wipe our rear ends'. At the time, I assumed they were simply very open about their bodily functions, but Bo 'Hok and Weng laughed at this interpretation and said that it was the women's way of indicating they were going fishing. Like fishing, *muee-loto* is an activity done in the river.

These guides were vague for other reasons. It used to frustrate me when they couldn't tell me how long it would take to arrive at a particular place that they knew well. The confusion arose from the fact that I was thinking in terms of miles and hours and they were thinking in terms of hunting. If there was a lot of game, a short distance could take a long time to cover because they would hunt. Equally, we could travel long distances quickly if there were no animals about or if they wanted to reach a place where they felt the hunting would be better. Their concept of distance was also dependent on mood or need. A destination 'not too far away' could mean a five-day walk through difficult terrain to a friendly village where they could buy tobacco. A 'long journey' might turn out to be a four-hour walk in the hated sunlight through flat farmland.

It was equally as difficult for them to understand my idea of time as it was for me to understand theirs. They took little interest in days and minutes and seconds. They were led by their moods and circumstances, whereas I was still controlled by my expectations.

ERIC NEWBY

# THE LAST GRAIN RACE

**T**HIRTEEN DAYS out from Spencer's Gulf we crossed the 180th meridian and suffered two Fridays in succession. Two Fridays were not popular. Sedelquist was angry because he had been deprived of the two Sundays he had hoped for; I was depressed because it meant an extra day of 'Backstern'; only Yonny Valker, that rigid medievalist, was happy, secure in the knowledge that here was a problem nobody would have the patience to explain to him.

'Koms to blow,' said Tria to me on the afternoon of the first Friday as I came on deck to pour the washing-up water over the side.

'Good.'

'No, no. Not good. Koms to blow bad,' he replied anxiously.

I asked him how he knew.

'I don' know how I know. There's someting fonny, someting noh good in the vind.' There was nobody about on the bridge deck, so I asked him if I could look at the last entry in the logbook in the charthouse.

'Orlright,' he said reluctantly. 'Don' let Kapten see you.' The Captain did not like finding the crew in the charthouse. I looked hastily at the open book and read the noon position:

'24.3.39. Lat. 51° 4S, Long. 176° 37′ 16W. Course East. Run 282. Barometer 4 a.m. 758 millimetres; Noon 754 millimetres. Wind WSW, Force 4.'

I glanced at the barometer. It had been falling steadily since

4 o'clock on Wednesday morning, the 22nd. On that day, except for some light northerly airs, we had been becalmed on a sea as grey and unvarying as a featureless plain. The albatross had vanished. At midnight on Wednesday the wind had been a gentle breeze from the NW. and by the afternoon of Thursday, the 23rd, *Moshulu* was logging 12 knots with WNW. wind, force 5. At 8 it had shifted to the west, the yards were squared, the spankers and the gaff topsail were taken in and she ran before it. The time was now 4 p.m. on the 24th, the wind WSW. The air was full of masses of white and grey cloud moving rapidly eastward above the ship, which was being driven and lifted forward with a slight see-saw motion on the crest of seas of immense depth and power. These seas did not seem to be raised by wind; instead they seemed the product of some widespread underwater convulsion. All round the ship the sea was surging and hurling itself into the air in plumes of spray, occasionally leaping over the rail by the mizzen braces and filling the main deck with a swirl of white water. The air was bitter; I could see Tria's breath smoking.

'It looks all right to me,' I said.

'I don' say right now,' said Tria. 'But very soon this blody ting gets so much as she can stand. Lissun when you go aloft.'

We were joined by the Sailmaker, who stood for some time looking up at the main royal with the wind straining in it, then over the rail at the mounting sea. 'Going to blow,' he said.

Hilbert came racing down the deck from the 'Vaskrum' for'ard, dressed in nothing but wooden clogs and fresh long underwear, his teeth chattering. All he said was: 'Vind,' and vanished into the starboard fo'c'sle. The First Mate looked down at us from deck. 'Going to vind a little too mooch,' he began conversationally.

'For Christ's sake,' I said, rather too audibly.

'What the hell are you doing?' he demanded, noticing me.

'Backstern, Sir.'

'Backstern doesn't take all bloddy day. Get down in the hold for babord'svakt for knacka rost.'

I went below to where the port watch were working suspended

on platforms over one of the 'tween-deck hatches. The only vacant space was next to Taanila, even more gnomelike than usual in goggles. I slipped in beside him and he turned as the platform gave a lurch. 'I tink . . .' he began. In that moment I wondered exactly what he was going to think. Was he going to think that I needed a knife inserted in some delicate part? Was he going to remind me yet again of my unfortunate nationality? Or was he going to tell me his opinion of 'knacka rost'?

'I tink it is going to . . .'

'Don't tell me, let me guess – to vind.'

'Yo, yo. How you know?'

'Because I'm bloody clever.'

At 5 the heavy chain sheet to the fore royal parted on the port side. We just managed to get the sail in before it blew itself to pieces. The remaining royals had to come in, and the flying jib, then all hands went aloft for the main and mizzen courses. All through the night there were two helmsmen. The wind increased and the seas rose higher and began to pour into the ship again. In the watch below I lay awake listening to the clang of freeing ports along the length of the main deck as they opened to the pressure of water and closed as the ship rolled away, tipping the sea right across her so that the same process took place on the other side. With more apprehension I listened to the sound of water trickling steadily into the fo'c'sle through a cracked port above Bäckmann's bunk. This seemed to constitute a far greater threat to our comfort than the more spectacular effects outside.

At 5.30 on the morning of the second Friday, *Moshulu*, still carrying her upper topgallants, began to labour under the onslaught of the heavy seas which were flooding on to the deck like a mill race. It was quite dark as six of us clewed-up the mizzen lower topgallant, and although from where I was at the tail of the rope I could see nothing at all except the hunched shoulders of Jansson ahead of me, I could hear Tria at the head of the line exhorting us. The sail was almost up when the wind fell quite suddenly and we all knew that we were in the trough of a wave far bigger than anything we had yet experienced. It was far too dark to see it at a distance, we could only sense its coming as the ship rolled slightly to port to meet it.

'Hoold . . .' someone began to shout as the darkness became darker still and the sea came looming over the rail. I was end man. There was just time to take a turn with the clewline round my middle and a good hold, the next moment it was on top of us. The rope was not torn from me; instead it was as though a gentle giant had smoothed his hands over my knuckles. They simply opened of their own accord and I unravelled from it like a cotton reel from the end of a thread and was swept away. As I went another body bumped me, and I received a blow in the eye from a seaboot. Then I was alone, rushing onwards and turning over and over. My head was filled with bright lights like a by-pass at night, and the air was full of the sounds of a large orchestra playing out of tune. In spite of this there was time to think and I thought: 'I'm done for.' At the same time the words of a sea poem, 'ten men hauling the lee fore brace . . . seven when she rose at last', came back to me with peculiar aptness. But only for an instant because now I was turning full somersaults, hitting myself violently again and again as I met something flat which might have been the coaming of No. 4 hatch, or the top of the charthouse, for all I knew. Then I was over it, full of water and very frightened, thinking 'Is this what it's like to drown?' No more obstructions now but still going very fast and still under water, perhaps no longer in the ship, washed overboard, alone in the Southern Ocean. Quite suddenly there was a parting of water, a terrific crash as my head hit something solid, and I felt myself aground.

Finding myself in the lee scuppers with my head forced right through a freeing port so that, the last of the great sea behind me spurted about my ears, I was in a panic that a second wave might come aboard and squeeze me through it like a sausage, to finish me off.

Staggering to my feet, my oilskins ballooning with water, too stupid from the blow on my head to be frightened, I had just enough sense to jump for the starboard lifeline when the next wave came boiling over the port quarter and obliterated everything from view.

Swinging above the deck on the lifeline with the sea sucking greedily at my boots, I began to realise what a fortunate escape I had had from serious injury, for the alacrity with which I had leapt for the lifeline in spite of the great weight of sea-water inside my oilskins had convinced me that I had suffered no damage except the bang on the head.

The sea had taken me and swept me from the pin rail of the mizzen rigging, where I had been working, diagonally across the deck for fifty feet past the Jarvis brace winches, on the long handles of which I could so easily have been speared, over the fife rails of the mizzen mast, right over the top of No. 3 hatch and into the scuppers by the main braces outside the Captain's quarters.

'Where you bin?' demanded Tria accusingly, when I managed to join the little knot of survivors who were forcing their way waist deep across the deck, spluttering, cursing, and spitting sea-water as they came.

'Paddling,' I said, relieved to find that there were still six of us.

'Orlright, don' be all bloody day,' he added unsympathetically.

'Tag I gigtåget. One more now. Ooh – ah, oh, bräck dem.'

'What happened?' I asked Jansson.

'That goddam Valker let her come up too mooch,' said Jansson. 'I bin all over the bloddy deck in that sea.'

On the second Friday *Moshulu*'s noon position was 50° 19′ S., 170° 36′ W. In 23½ hours she had sailed 296 miles.* This was the best day's sailing with cargo she ever had with Erikson. It was only bettered by the Germans on very few occasions. Twice in 1909 on a voyage from Newcastle, N.S.W., to Valparaiso when loaded with nearly 5,000 tons of coal she ran 300 miles.

At midnight the wind was SW., force 6, and in the early hours of Saturday morning I went aloft with Hermansonn in a storm of sleet to make fast the main upper topgallant. It was now blowing a fresh gale, force 8, and the yard was swinging like a mad thing; we had a terrible time with this sail. Some of the gaskets had been

---

* When running to the east in southerly latitudes a day, noon to noon, is about 23½ hours.

caught in the buntline blocks on the yard and were immovable, others were missing. The sleet numbed our fingers until we almost cried with cold.

Below us, in the fore and mizzen rigging, eight boys were having the time of their lives furling the lower topgallants; on the mizzen two buntlines had carried away to starboard and the sail was being clewed-up to the yard with lines taken to the capstan on the main deck, where from time to time ton upon ton of white water poured over the rail, causing those heaving at the capstan bars to abandon their efforts and leap for the lifelines.

'OOH, what bloddy cold,' screamed Hermansonn. 'Ut, Kossuri, you strongbody, you rosbif, ut, ut på nock.'

As we reached the yardarm there was a great ripping sound that seemed to come from below, and we both hung dizzily over the yard to see whether the upper topsail had blown out. Then, in spite of the wind and our precarious situation, Hermansonn began to laugh. I knew then that I had suffered some dire misfortune as Hermansonn only laughed in that way when a disaster happened to someone else.

'Ho, ho!' he boomed above the gale. 'Ho, ho, focking fonny!'

'What?' I screamed in his ear. 'Tell me.'

'Your trousers, ho, ho. English, no good.'

It was true. My oilskin trousers, unable to stand the strain to which they had been subjected, had split from end to end.

This was an accident of the worst kind. To find myself halfway across the Southern Ocean, in the stormiest seas in the world, with defective oilskin trousers, was a calamity.

At the moment however there was no time to worry over such things. The wind was awe-inspiring. Not only was it so strong in the gusts that we could do nothing but hang on until it lessened, but it moaned in a way which I had never heard before, rising and falling like the winds heard about old houses in the wintertime. It seemed, in spite of its force, to be the last part of some even more violent disturbance that was taking place at a great distance. This then was what Tria had meant when he told me to listen when I went aloft.

But in this weather there were still worse jobs on deck where the Carpenter and two helpers were trying to caulk the closet. As the ship started to run downhill into the valley between two seas, she would bury her bows nearly to the fo'c'sle head, so that the water surged into the pipes and shot into the compartment in a solid icy column like the jet emitted by a whale, leaving them half drowned and spluttering.

At noon the wind was WSW., force 9, and there was a vicious sea running. We were carrying upper and lower topsails, the fore-sail, forestaysail and jigger staysail. I spent the morning with a sail-needle, seaming up my ruined oilskins, while overhead the starboard watch struggled to reeve fresh buntlines on the mizzen lower topgallant. The outer steel doors of the fo'c'sle were fast, but not being close-fitting they let the water in. Soon there were more than six inches of water in the compartment reserved for our seaboots and oilskins, and half as much in the fo'c'sle itself. Every few minutes I had to leave my stitching and bail with a cocoa tin to prevent the fo'c'sle being flooded still more. Everyone else was asleep. As old soldiers do before an action, they were absorbing sleep greedily like medicine, and lay snoring happily in the midst of tumult.

For the noise was unbelievable. In the fo'c'sle the shrieking of the wind through the shrouds and about the upper yards now bereft of sail, so awe-inspiring on the open decks, was here only a murmur subordinated to the shuddering and groaning of the hull under stress and to the sounds of water; water thundering over the ship in torrents, water sluicing out through the freeing ports, water trickling into the fo'c'sle in half-a-dozen different ways, and sloshing about the floor.

By the time I had mended the trousers, the free watch was nearly over. I was 'Backstern', and having made sure that Kroner had put on the washing-up water, I waited for a lull to dash forward to the fo'c'sle head from where I could look back along the ship.

*Moshulu* was running ten knots in the biggest seas I had ever seen. As I watched, the poop began to sink before my eyes and the horizon astern was blotted out by a high polished wall, solid and impenetrable like marble. The poop went on dropping until the whole ship seemed to be toppling backwards into the deep moat below the wall of water that loomed over her, down and down to the bottom of the sea itself. At the moment when it seemed that this impregnable mass must engulf us, a rift appeared in its face and it collapsed beneath the ship, bearing her up so that what a moment before seemed a sluggish, solid hulk destined for the sea bed was now like a bird skimming the water, supported by the wind high above the valley.

This was noon.

In the first part of the afternoon the barometer was low, 742 millimetres. At one moment *Moshulu* would be riding the crests in brilliant sunshine, the next swooping down a great incline of water peppered by rain and hailstones, yawing a little from her course and beginning to roll, taking sea as high as her charthouse. Everyone was soaking wet and none of us had any more dry clothes. Everything in the Vuitton was wet as well. All through the afternoon we were kept busy making new wire buntlines, cold work with no movement in it, but by coffee-time one of my shirts had dried over the galley fire and I put it on rejoicing. But not for long.

As soon as I came out on deck I heard a voice calling me. It was the Captain, in leather coat and tweed cap, like a huge backwoods peer I had seen in a *Tatler* that the Sailmaker had somehow saved from destruction.

'Here you,' he said. 'Take up some slack on the crojack sheet.'

I plunged down on to the maindeck, where I was immediately knocked flat by a sea coming inboard. After this initial soaking, I no longer cared whether I was wet or not, only leaping for the lifelines when big dangerous seas came aboard.

At six there was a slight easing in the wind. I happened to be coming from the wheel, when once more the Captain had something in mind for me.

'We'll see what she can stand,' he said in a speculative way, like a gambler about to stake a large sum on an uncertainty.

'Aloft and break out the main lower topgallant. Lively now.' As I went I heard Sedelquist, who had been at the wheel with me, say: 'Crazy focker.' Privately agreeing with him, I swung myself on to the pin rail and into the main rigging. Aloft the wind seemed as strong as ever, and I looked down to a deck as narrow as a ruler on which the tiny figures of the watch were clustered, waiting to perform the ticklish job of sheeting home the sail which I was about to loose from its gaskets.

A distant cry borne on the wind told me that they were ready.

I cast off the gaskets on the weather side, hauled up a good slack on the buntlines, and, scuttling into the rigging, clung to the shrouds for my life. The yard began to plunge and whip, the bunt-lines plucked at the blocks seized to the shrouds, making the rat-lines tremble underfoot.

'She'll never stand it,' was the general verdict when I regained the deck.

With the sail sheeted home there was too much strain on the entire sail structure and at eight o'clock the upper topsail sheet carried away and the sail had to be taken in, together with the lower topgallant we had recently set.

Thus reduced, we drove on in the darkness with both topsails set on the fore and mizzen, the main lower topsail, the foresail and one fore-and-aft sail – the jigger staysail.

This was the night of the second Friday, March 24th. We were fed up and though we cursed *Moshulu* and the Captain too, we were pleased with him for pushing her to the limit.

DEA BIRKETT

# SERPENT IN PARADISE

*C*AN'T PLAN for the future here,' said Ben, working on the finger-nails of his hand vase. We had been sitting on the veranda all afternoon, and still no news of when the ship would call.

'Can't plan for future on Pitcairn.' Ben often said the same sentence twice, slightly rephrased, as if he expected to be misunderstood, or ignored.

Terry was listening, but made no outward sign of having heard.

Then he began. '*Willem Ruys* due to stop 26th April, a Friday, 1963, with one thousand passengers. We work very hard on souvenirs. Day before she due, Thursday 25th, news come through. Weather so bad that ha ship far behind. She no stopping.'

We sat for a further five minutes or more without speaking.

'What you doing, Terry?' I asked.

'Jus waiting.'

Ben looked up. 'When ha ship comen, you jus wait around.'

The following afternoon the bell struck five times. We had been waiting on the veranda, the bike loaded with bananas, since the previous day. But now the starting gun had been fired and we were off. Within minutes we were down at the Landing and we jumped into *Tub*, followed by our baskets of curios and Dennis's mail bags containing my postcard home.

Wrapped in newspaper in my new curio basket was one of Ben's hand vases, with his signature scratched on the base by Irma, and three small sharks from Dennis. I had a notion to see if the chief steward had any garlic, to swap for some postcards or stamps.

The *Erickson Frost* rose over the horizon and roller-coastered towards us, as broad and high as a tidal wave. Yet Steve kept us bobbing towards her, the engine on full throttle, as if a meeting of equals, not a tiny longboat heading for a rampart of steel. When all we could see was the side of the ship, Steve dance-stepped *Tub* sideways, and we attached ourselves to her.

The wall of faces at the top of the rope ladder was a familiar formation – one group short, dark and round faced, smiling and constantly moving; the other tall, silver-blond, with arms crossed and sage expressions. Filipino crew and Scandinavian officers, standing either side at the top of the rope ladder.

The sea was so calm that I skipped on to the rung, and skittled up.

'That's dangerous,' said an officer, crossing his arms even tighter and rocking from side to side on large, flat, booted feet. When he stopped speaking, the rocking was arrested and he became a statue of Viking virtues again.

I sniffed. 'You just have to watch for the swell. Whe're you bound?'

'New Zealand.' The officer was not a talkative man.

'What are you carrying?' I tried to counter his taciturnity with a light skip in my voice.

'Ba-na-nas.' Bananas acted as a rhythm for the officer's rocking – right (ba), left (na), right (nas).

'Anything else?'

'No. Only ba-na-nas.'

'Would you show me to the galley, please?'

He thumbed aft, then recrossed his arms.

'Thanks.'

The *Erickson Frost* seemed very large, much larger than I remembered the *Tundra Queen*. But perhaps my vision had shrunk. Fish and people came in extra-large on Pitcairn, but everything else was a child-sized portion.

I must have walked to Tedside and back just reaching the galley. And the galley itself was not one big room, but a series of utilitarian, uncluttered spaces, through several of which was the chief steward by a row of cold stores.

'Hello. How do you do?' I fanned out some postcards. 'Do you lave any garlic, please?'

He nodded enthusiastically – 'Please, please' – unbolted a cold store and showed me inside. Although it was no bigger than a large cupboard, he followed me in, and stood close to me among the sacks of vegetables – red onions, sweet peppers, cabbages, whose leaves were already curling, and Irish tatties. There was a netting bag of garlic bulbs, tied together in bunches; the chief steward reached in and picked out a big bunch for me. He waved the bunch before his face as if displaying a shrunken head, then closed the door.

My first thought was: *it's very cold in here.* My second: *you're smaller than me,* as the chief steward made a lunge towards me. He pulled me to his chest and attempted to kiss me, jerking my head towards his. I tugged my head away and kicked his shins. He stood back a moment, and we confronted each other in the cold room, like boxers just before the bell for the next round.

*Ding!* And the chief steward lunged towards me again, this time adopting the tactic of holding my arms down and pushing me up against the cold steel door.

I shouted, 'What the fuck–', freed an arm and walloped him in the face. It was the shock, not the force of my blow that made him totter away from me. And, as if insulted, he touched his struck cheek softly. Then he smiled at me.

'Please,' he said, grinning broadly, making the word as long as a snake. He was still holding the bunch of garlic in one hand, and waved it at me, as if enticing a dog with a bit of fine meat. Then he pointed towards a sack of onions.

'You would like?'

'No, I would not like your fucking onions!'

*Ding!* He pushed at my shoulder so I fell back. He kissed my shoulder, then started to make a line of kisses towards my mouth.

It felt like a cockroach crawling up my neck. I wriggled and kicked, but it didn't deter him. It began to dawn on me that he actually liked it. I could feel the bunch of garlic – clasped in his hand – banging against the top of my leg.

I began to draw circles away from myself; first, there was the cold room with its sack of red onions, its peppers, its Irish tatties, all stacked about me as the chief steward splattered my neck with kisses. Beyond that was the galley, where Jay would be striking a bargain for his frozen snapper. Beyond that was the deck where Royal, Nola, Kari and Meralda had their curios spread out on a sheet before them. There was Dennis on the bridge offering the captain our bunches of bananas, while the hold below held thousands of tons of the same fruit. Glen would be keeping the helm in the longboat as she floated alongside. Beyond that was the reach of sea to Bounty Bay, the pimple of rock called Pitcairn, and then the great ocean. Three thousand miles away was New Zealand, where the *Erickson Frost* with her chief steward on board were bound.

With renewed energy, I threw the chief steward off. We tussled with each other, I pulled his hair, kicked him, and he sneaked kisses whenever a piece of my flesh was close enough to his. I had the sense that he thought this was all part of a game, and that despite my show of resistance, a bargain had been struck: I would let him have rough-'n'-tumble sex with me in exchange for a bunch of garlic bulbs. I wondered for how long this would go on; would we continue for hours, throwing each other against the sacks of onions until the red peels began to crumble? Would we, exhausted by the fight, collapse in a heap, panting and dewed from the cold? Would the longboat leave without me, as I sailed on in the cold room to Auckland?

'FUCK YOUUUUUUUU!' I delivered one last blow. It hit the chief steward on the forearm, and his hand shot up smartly as if from an electric shock.

'Ooooh.' It was more an expression of surprise than pain. He looked at me with utter disgust, sized up what our encounter had been worth, picked off one bulb of garlic from the bunch, and threw it at me. It hit my chest and fell on the floor. I walked over to the sacks, held out my sweatshirt as an apron, and filled it with onions. I nodded towards the door, and the chief steward drew it back and let me through.

It was warm and bright in the galley. Jay was offering some fish for a drum of sunflower oil. He saw my hammock of onions and the chief steward close behind, and winked.

We were making ready to leave. Baskets and the drum of sunflower oil were lowered on ropes, knocking against the side. Steve was handling a large television, which he had exchanged for twelve Pitcairn T-shirts. Large plastic sacks marked Hazardous Waste were bundled into the longboat.

'What's that?' I asked Kari, hanging over the deckrail.

'Later. I tell you later,' and she reached for a rope for her curio basket.

I climbed down the ladder as the longboat lounged on a quiet sea. Trade had been good, so the singing was heartfelt.

> *We part, but hope to meet again*
> *Goodbye, goodbye, goodbye.*

I turned to Randy, Trent's younger brother, who was sitting next to me. 'The ship looks so huge,' I said. 'There's nothing that size on Pitcairn.'

'The island,' he said, bluntly.

Although there was a swell, the mood on board was buoyant and not even Betty was seasick.

'Onions!' said Royal, peering into my bag.

'Fucking onions,' I said, and Royal laughed. It was the first time I had cracked a joke on Pitcairn.

WHIT DESCHNER

# TRAVELS WITH A KAYAK

O N ONE OF Captain Cook's visits to New Zealand, he dropped off – much to the crew's delight – a bunch of pigs. Supposedly the pigs were to help feed ship-wrecked survivors. This made the Maoris extremely happy, for it offered them a change of menu from the usual, ship-wrecked survivor. Not only was the pork more tender, but the pigs were also easier to clean. Yet the arrangement also must have confused the Maoris. What were they to think of a culture that said, 'Well, instead of improving navigation, we'll just drop pigs off all over the world where our ships are going to crash . . .' Probably the same thing the British would have thought had the Maoris landed in Great Britain and dropped off canoe-loads of moas.

In the remote regions of the North Island, the pigs still run feral. In theory this seems a sound idea, since these regions also contain some good kayaking and the chances of wrecking or losing a boat are also good. You know, sort of the modern, twentieth-century shipwreck. But any kayak-wrecked survivor who thinks he is going to step into the bush and subsist on bacon is a kayaker with a serious brain malfunction. The pigs that survive come from a genetically enhanced line, a strain that learned to outrun Maoris.

One of the largest natural* pig habitats in the country is around the East Cape region, specifically the Motu River. Although the

* As opposed to Auckland

upper reaches of this river are pastoral and sheep-infested – which probably accounts for the river's wonderful murky-green hue – the lower fifty-five-mile section has hills crowding it that are referred to as mountains. Whether these *are* mountains or not, I'm not going to argue. I do know, however, that the Tarzan-oriented vegetation that smothers them would severely hinder an escape from the valley, unless you are adept at swinging on vines.

My escape, though, was to the valley. Carol and I were hiding from Christmas. Now, don't get me wrong about Christmas. There's nothing I like better than the slow pace of a good Christmas traffic jam to bring my fellow man good cheer and, as he fights to buy the last Nintendo, peace on earth. I dread to think what the leading economic indicators would do if we returned to the old standard of sleigh bells ringing instead of cash registers. As a protest, I used to send my Christmas cards out in the middle of summer, an idea I thought original to the point of genius. However, my enthusiasm was totally squashed one day when I realised that *everyone* in the southern hemisphere sends their Christmas cards out in the middle of summer. And, as I subsequently discovered, the temperate climate in New Zealand has totally mutated the holiday season. In an eighty-degree environment, fake snow in the corner of store windows is hardly convincing. Santa in his winter garb looks like the perfect S-and-M perversion. His most famous quote, 'Ho, ho, ho,' sounds more like the mournful last gasps of a person locked in a sauna.

So on our escape, setting off down the Motu River, we made a pact not even to mention the big C-word. As for the run itself, providing a flood didn't drown us and wash us into the Bay of Plenty (plenty of what, no one could say, but I suspect kayak gear) the river promised some classic whitewater. Actually, the river didn't promise this; some boaters who told us to run it did. So did the local guidebook.

That book also advised there was virtually no camping for the first seventeen miles as the river went through two gorges. Now, when I think of two gorges I think of one gorge followed by another gorge, with some ungorge-like behaviour in between. Not in this upper section. Here space for gorges is at a premium; the two are smunched together so close it takes a geologist with a magnifying glass to detect the difference.

Flooding was also noted, both by the guidebook and myself: a scoured no-man's land rose twenty to thirty feet above the currently non-flooding river. In one recorded instance, the river had, overnight, gone from forty cubic feet a second to *six thousand*. But the guide's most notable item was this little gem, an extra incentive not to miss a roll: *'Motu eels deserve special mention – many as thick as a man's leg and they seem to be exceedingly hungry. It is not advisable to be in the water after dark as they have been known to attack humans at this time.'*

The river was just cloudy enough to obscure my view of the life that I knew was lurking within it, feeding my suspicions that only an all-too-thin layer of fibreglass separated my personal rump steak from a river teeming with eels, the bigger ones no doubt inhabiting the pools below nastier rapids.

In short, the price we were paying to escape Christmas was to share a large, flood-prone trench all day with eels giant enough to star in their own Hollywood horror flick. But these were just abstract and potential problems, nothing like the real one that developed as we descended. Due to various uncharted rocks, our boats began leaking. They were only a week old and now, quite literally, we were breaking them in. When ordering the kayaks, I had specified heavy-duty. They were fifty pounds each so the first criterion had been met, but the 'duty' was neglected. In a matter of hours the boats were wearing half a roll of duct tape between them. Ironically, we were carrying a dozen raw eggs packed only in their cardboard container and *not one* of them cracked. Pulling ashore to fix another hole, I kicked my boat and immediately had another crack to repair. With four-and-a-half days yet to go on a rapidly diminishing roll of tape, it looked like we might be hunting pigs after all. But it was darkly comforting to know we were not the only people who had suffered such a problem. At the river's hardest drop, 'The Slot', we discovered two wrecked kayaks abandoned in the brush; they were the same make, the same pie-crust construction.

We reached camp at dusk, just as the exceedingly hungry leg-sized eels no doubt began prowling the river, cruising for kayakers foolish enough to linger in the water.

The next day the valley temporarily yawned and vegetation, not rock, flanked the river. One such plant was the cabbage tree, a Dr Suess designer plant. Around forty-feet tall, these trees contained no foliage except for a single cluster at the end of each branch. We also saw the rare, dove-grey blue mountain ducks. Crouching along the river's edge as we passed, they apparently believed they were going unnoticed – which is, of course, the reason why they are rare.

After floating a handful of miles we came to a permanent camp and would have passed right by had it not been for a ribbon of smoke advertising someone's presence. We stopped, hoping for some river information.

The camp's lone occupant met us as we stepped from our boats. He said, 'I really don't like boaters coming ashore here, I've got cyanide all over the place.'

'Cyanide?'

'For trapping possums. It's horrible stuff. They scream when they die.'

'That's OK,' I said. 'We'll shove back off. We were just wondering what you knew about the river.'

'It bloody well nearly flooded me out of my own camp.'

'You know anything about it downstream?'

'Nothing but bloody waterfalls and whirlpools!'

'You've seen it then?'

'No way! The kayakers told me. I wouldn't go near it. The bloody thing's filled with eels.'

'Well, thanks. We'll be going.'

'You'd better have a cuppa tea first.'

After emptying six cups of tea and supersaturating our kidneys close to failure, Carol and I learned the trapper's name was Beaver. While Carol and I were eluding Christmas, Beaver was eluding most concepts of civilisation – like washing. And as much as he espoused the life of a recluse, he sure seemed starved for company. Every time we finished our tea, Beaver snatched the tea billy from the coals and refilled our cups.

Whenever we asked anything about the outside world or his past, Beaver became vague, as if suffering from mild amnesia. But when we asked him about life in the bush we couldn't shut him up. Like only yesterday, walking his trap line, he'd unknowingly stepped between a wild sow and her piglets. The sow charged. Having only a single shot .22, he had to be certain that his bullet wouldn't stray. He shot the pig at ten feet; it dropped dead at his feet. He said we'd have it for 'tea'.

'But we've got to be going,' I insisted.

'It's only going to go to waste if you don't stay.' Then he asked what day it was.

'December twenty-fourth,' I said.

'I thought so,' he said sadly, but then, in the same breath and a revived eagerness, added, 'it'll be our Christmas pork.'

I helped him fetch the carcass, which was in a gunny sack, but the flies had got to it anyway and blown all but a shoulder. After carving the good meat off, he asked, 'You seen any eels yet?'

'Not yet.'

'I'll show you bloody eels!'

We carried the carcass down to the water's edge, Beaver tied a line around a leg, tied the line to the bank, and pushed the remains into the river.

That evening pork hissed in the frying pan. We gorged ourselves then lay back, watching the darkness push the evening pastels from the sky. At last, when the stars were out in full bloom, we checked the carcass. We trooped down to the river's edge and Beaver, holding a kerosene lantern aloft, proclaimed, 'That's why I don't go swimming in the bloody river!' I could hardly see the carcass for all the eels dangling from it. I leaped to a boulder for a closer look, not seeing that the boulder was slimy and that a foot would never adhere to it. My momentum carried me into the water, landing me squarely on the carcass. All I was wearing were shorts. All I felt were eels slithering over my body. Jesus might have walked on water, but I ran.

The next morning – each of us carefully avoiding any mention of what day it was – Beaver cooked up more pork. Tea, of course, washed it down, and when our cups were empty we insisted they not be refilled, that we really had to be leaving.

Carol asked Beaver for an address where she could send him a card but he sadly admitted he didn't have one. So we thanked him, wished him luck, and floated away – but not before noticing the pig carcass stripped clean.

We paddled the remaining gorge. It was wider and less technical; with the greater volume there was little worry about adding additional holes to our boats. However, in this section helmets became an essential piece of equipment; as they scrambled for safety, the wild goats on the cliffs were forever showering us with rocks. When we came to the end of the gorge, we camped. That evening, as we ate dinner, clouds crowded across the sky and shortly afterwards it began to sprinkle. We went to bed.

When the drizzle stopped I awoke, immediately becoming aware of a strange twinkling. Looking out the tent screen, I saw the whole valley aglow with dim fairy-like lights. I said, 'Carol, wake up.'

'Why?'

'Are you awake?'

'No.'

'I won't say what day it still is, but look outside.'

We stayed awake for the rest of Christmas gazing at hundreds of glow worms clinging to the nooks of the cliffs.

I wish this story ended there, but it doesn't. Several months later while staying with a friend I told him of our trip down the Motu and of the possum trapper we'd stayed with. He said, 'You say, possum trapper?'

Then he began to dig through a pile of newspapers until he found the article he wanted me to read. It was about an escaped convict who had been hiding out in the Motu Valley. The police had finally caught up with him.

## ROBYN DAVIDSON

# TRACKS

**T**HAT EVENING the camels played in the white dust, raising balloons of cloud that the fat, red setting sun caught, burst and turned to gold. I lay on a foot-thick mattress of fallen leaves which scattered golden jangles of firelight in a thousand directions. Night calls and leaf sighs floated down to me on the breeze and around me was a cathedral of black and silver giant ghost-gums, the thin sliver of platinum moon cradled in their branches. The heart of the world had been found. I drifted into sleep in that palace and allowed the mountains to fade along the rim of my mind. The heart of the world, paradise.

I decided to stay in that place as long as the water held out. Rick and responsibilities were so far away from me now, so remote, I didn't give them a moment's consideration. I planned to enter the sandhills and ride out to those distant mountains. But first the camels must rest. There was feed here to burn. Saltbush, camel thorn, mulga, everything their little hearts could desire. Diggity and I explored. We found a cave in Pine Ridge which had Aboriginal paintings plastered all over it. Then we climbed up a narrow, treacherous rocky gap, the wind howling and whistling down at us. We pulled ourselves up to the flat top, where freakish rock strata ran in great buttresses and giant steps. The trees up there were gnarled into crippled shapes by the roar of the wind. Along the distant horizon I could see a sandstorm being whipped up into a cloud of red, straight out of *Beau Geste*. Further west, we discovered ancient desert palms, called black-boys. Rough black stumps shooting out fountains of green needles at the top, all huddled together by themselves, like an alien race left behind on a forgotten planet. There was a haunting hallucinatory quality about this place. I felt swelled by it, high as a kite. I was filled with an emotion I had not felt before – joy.

Those days were like a crystallisation of all that had been good in the trip. It was as close to perfection as I could ever hope to come. I reviewed what I had learnt. I had discovered capabilities and strengths that I would not have imagined possible in those distant dream-like days before the trip. I had rediscovered people in my past and come to terms with my feelings towards them. I had learnt what love was. That love wanted the best possible for those you cared for even if that excluded yourself. That before, I had wanted to possess people without loving them, and now I could love them and wish them the best without needing them. I had understood freedom and security. The need to rattle the foundations of habit. That to be free one needs constant and unrelenting vigilance over one's weaknesses. A vigilance which requires a moral energy most of us are incapable of manufacturing. We relax back into the moulds of habit. They are secure, they bind us and keep us contained at the expense of freedom. To break the moulds, to be heedless of the seductions of security is an impossible struggle, but one of the few that count. To be free is to learn, to test yourself constantly, to gamble. It is not safe. I had learnt to use my fears as stepping stones rather than stumbling blocks, and best of all I had learnt to laugh. I felt invincible, untouchable, I had extended myself, and I believed I could now sit back, there was nothing else the desert could teach me. And I wanted to remember all this. Wanted to remember this place and what it meant to me, and how I had arrived there. Wanted to fix it so firmly in my head that I would never, ever forget.

In the spast, my bouts of gloom and despair had led, like widdershins,* to the same place. And it seemed that at that place was a signpost saying, 'Here it is', here is the thing you must push through, leap free of, before you can learn any more. It was as if

* water-worn gulleys

the self brought me constantly to this place – took every opportunity to show it to me. It was as if there was a button there which I could push if I only had the courage. If I could only just remember. Ah, but we always forget. Or are too lazy. Or too frightened. Or too certain we have all the time in the world. And so back up the ravines to the comfortable places (the sane ones?) where we don't have to think too much. Where life is, after all, just 'getting by' and where we survive, half asleep.

And I thought I had done it. I believed I had generated a magic for myself that had nothing to do with coincidence, believed I was part of a strange and powerful sequence of events called fate and I was beyond the need for anything or anyone. And that night I received the most profound and cruel lesson of all. That death is sudden and final and comes from nowhere. It had waited for my moment of supreme complacency and then it had struck. Late that night, Diggity took a poison bait.

We were running low on dog food, and I was too lazy, too high to want to go and shoot her game. So I rationed her. She woke me up sneaking sheepishly back into the swag. 'What's up, Dig, where've you been, little woofing?' She licked my face profusely, snuffled her way under the covers, and snuggled as usual into my belly. I cuddled her. Suddenly she slunk out again and began to vomit. My body went cold. 'Oh no, no it can't be, please, Jesus, not this.' She came back to me and licked my face again. 'It's OK, Dig, you're just a little bit sick. Don't worry, little one, you come and snuggle in here and get warm and you'll be OK in the morning.' Within minutes she was out again. This couldn't be happening. She was my little dog and she couldn't be poisoned. That was impossible, couldn't happen to her. I got up to check what she had brought up. I remember trembling uncontrollably and droning to her, 'It's all right, Dig, everything's all right, don't worry,' over and over. She had eaten some dead animal but it didn't smell rotten, so I repeated to myself that she couldn't be poisoned. I forced myself to believe yet I knew it wasn't true. My head raced through what you do for strychnine poisoning. You have to swing them around your head to make them get rid of it all, but even if you do it immediately there's virtually no chance of survival. 'Well, I won't do that anyway, because you're not poisoned, you're not poisoned. You're my Dig and it can't happen to you.' Diggity started wandering around retching violently and coming back to me for reassurance. She knew. Suddenly she ran away to some black acacia bushes and turned to face me. She barked and howled at me and I knew she must be hallucinating, knew she was dying. Her two mirror eyes burnt an image into my brain that will not fade. She came over to me and put her head between my legs. I picked her up and swung her round my head. Round and round and round. She kicked and struggled. I tried to pretend it was a game. I let her down and she went crashing through the undergrowth barking like a mad dog. I raced for the gun, I loaded it and went back. She was on her side convulsing. I blew her brains out. I knelt frozen like that for a long time then I staggered back to the swag and got in. My body shook with uncontrollable spasms. I vomited. Sweat soaked into the pillow and blankets. I thought I was dying too. I thought that when she licked me, I had swallowed some strychnine. 'Is this what it feels like to die? Am I dying? No, no, it's just shock, stop it, you must go to sleep.' I've never been able before or since to do what I did then. I shut my brain off and willed it into immediate unconsciousness.

I woke well before dawn. The sick, steely, pre-dawn light was enough to find the things I needed. I caught the camels and gave them some water. I packed my belongings and loaded up and forced myself to drink some water. I felt nothing. Then suddenly it was time to leave that place and I didn't know what to do. I had a profound desire to bury the dog. I told myself it was ridiculous. It was natural and correct for the body to decay on the surface of the ground. But there was an overwhelming need in me to ritualise, to make real and tangible what had happened. I walked back to Diggity's body, stared at it, and tried to make all of myself face what was there. I didn't bury her. But I said goodbye to a creature I had loved unconditionally, without question. I said my goodbyes and my thank-yous and I wept for the first time and covered the body with a handful of fallen leaves. I walked out into the morning and felt nothing. I was numb, empty. All I knew was I mustn't stop walking.

# ANTARCTICA

DEBORAH SHAPIRO AND ROLF BJELKE

# TIME ON ICE
## A Winter Voyage to Antarctica

**T**HE MONTH continues to be windy. On August 12, we wake in the middle of the night with a feeling that the Booth Island 'weather dam' has just broken. Until minutes ago the boat was frozen fast in three-foot-thick ice, but now it's vibrating so violently that our mattress is moving around. It feels like a giant has grabbed our mainmast and is shaking the boat as hard as he can.

As I get up, I think about how unusually high the barometric pressure was a week ago: 1,015 millibars. Since then, the pressure dropped continuously for six days, a fair warning that a lot of wind was on its way. I turn on the spreader lights, but I can't see well through the cupola because it's almost entirely snowed over. I can only see out aft, and there everything is a grey haze. The wind is coming from dead ahead at an average well above 60 knots, and the roar generated in the rigging is deafening. I wait until the wind finally decreases a little before opening the cupola to look forward. Through the driving snow I manage to see that the cause of the shaking is the forestay swinging from side to side, moving almost three feet in each direction.

While I dress to go outdoors, layering on the warmest of my winter gear, I think about how we felt two months ago when the boat froze fast. Deborah and I figured we had a long vacation ahead of us; we neither could nor needed to do anything for the boat. The thicker the ice became, the safer and more secure we felt. For weeks now the boat has been sitting so steady in the ice that we could have let the shore lines go and still stayed put. It felt like living on shore. Until just a few minutes ago, our dream about a long, relaxing time without boat responsibilities was fulfilled in every respect. That's not to say that it hadn't been windy already, but nothing like this had occurred.

By the time I have my anorak on, the shaking has become so violent that it is apparent I need to hurry. Something in the rigging will soon give up.

As I wait for the proper time to open the cupola, my mind races. I assume the swaying begins when the forestay profile's leading edge is turned into the wind and its aerodynamic shape develops lift. If my theory is correct, then turning the profile sideways to the wind should stop the phenomenon. But outside, as I am hit by the first gust, I recall that long ago, to make it easier to shovel snow, we removed all lines leading to the cockpit, including the one from the furling jib. To turn the profile, I'll have to make my way out to it on the bowsprit.

There is so much snow in the air that I have to make my way by feel. To avoid the bone-chilling wind, I lower myself into a crouch. The last bit across the foredeck can only be safely accomplished on all fours. I eventually get out on the bowsprit and turn the profile. The swaying does stop, but not for long. The wind is never so constant in direction for there to be one perfect resting position for the profile. No matter how I position it, it's just a matter of time until the swaying starts again.

I look around. Despite the deck lights, it is impossible in the dark to judge what is below me. I can barely make out the teak grating my knees are resting on. The driving spindrift makes it look as if the boat is rushing through the darkness at a dizzying speed. The cold is numbing, windchill hastening its effect. I begin to have difficulty thinking. As soon as I look up, snow stings my face. Time and motions start to seem dragged out.

The force of the wind and shaking become so violent that the whole bowsprit starts pumping. Finally, I come up with a possible solution. What if I attach the genoa halyard to the pulpit on the starboard side? Perhaps that's the answer.

Surprisingly, I manage to open the frozen hank. I unwrap the halyard from the profile and then take a couple of turns around the pulpit and secure it. Then I work my way to the mainmast, where I tension the line with the help of the halyard winch. The result of running the genoa halyard almost parallel to the forestay profile is that a slot effect creates a low pressure and the halyard and profile are drawn toward each other. The swaying stops. But the peace doesn't last long this time either. In the next gust, the wind shifts again, enough to start the pumping all over again.

Still, I believe I'm on track. To complete the arrangement, I release the spinnaker halyard hank from the mainmast. My plan is to attach it dead ahead of the furling profile and by doing so create a similar slot effect to the genoa halyard's. I pull at least four yards more slack in the halyard than necessary for the distance, but the wind grabs the rope with such force that I can only pull it as far as the bow. There, I wrap the halyard around the cutter stay a few turns and use both hands to hold on. When the wind finally 'eases' momentarily, I continue out on to the bowsprit. Eventually I fasten the halyard where I want it. Back at the mast, I winch it tight and all the swaying stops. I wait a few anxious minutes before I am certain the problem has indeed been solved. Satisfied, I make my way aft to the cockpit and down into the boat.

'That was an unexpected manoeuvre,' Deborah says, then she takes my arm and smiles. She is just as relieved as I am that I am back safely. 'But gee, it took you a long time. Just tightening up two halyards took four times as long as it used to take you to change headsails,' she says. I look at the clock. 'Whew, that actually took me a whole hour?' I ask.

I should've known better than to take the bait. Deborah nods and says, 'Yes, you must be getting old.' I don't bother commenting. I'll show her how wrong she is.

A few hours later nature interrupts our sleep again, this time with a terrible jolt. Before we even understand what is happening, the boat heels so much that I roll into Deborah, and together we continue gliding off the mattress up on to the side of the hull. An eternity passes before the boat ever starts to righten, and during that time we try our best to crawl out of bed. But at the same speed we crawl uphill, the mattress slides farther to the lee. When we finally reach the floorboards and are on our way out into the galley, the boat is almost upright. Then it's forced over again, this time to starboard, with such force that both of us are nearly knocked over.

The floor is suddenly covered with items that have been standing on counters for months. It is difficult to know where to put our bare feet. We must be particularly careful to not step on anything sharp. When I eventually reach a light switch, we see on the clinometer that the boat is heeling 25 degrees.

It takes half a minute before the boat starts to righten, but this time it never comes all the way up. One violent gust is quickly replaced by another. As soon as wind comes from 5 to 10 degrees off the bow, the boat is completely knocked over again. The force this wind must have is difficult to fathom.

Each time the boat hits the edge of the ice, anything that can move inside the boat does. Saucepans, utensils, glasses and plates shift in lockers and drawers. The cans in the bilge roll. The cumulative cacophony is amazing. It sounds like no one thing will survive intact. The wind must have increased to far over hurricane force. The worst gusts shriek somewhere between 90 and 120 knots.

There's nothing else to do but crawl back under the blanket. But it's impossible to sleep, and not just because of the noise of the thunks and crashes each time the boat twists or lurches in its ice cradle. We start to wonder what kind of damage the boat may be incurring. We know it would be insane to go out now to try to look, but we hope that by the time it gets light the wind will have decreased some. What worries me most is that the log propeller and the rudder can break or bend as the boat rolls against the ice.

That thought is not more than finished before we hear a terrible bang. This time the noise comes from the stern. Each time the boat heels, it bangs again. We recognise the noise; the tiller is hitting a bollard. That means that the steering wire connecting the wheel to the tiller has snapped.

In the early part of the winter when the ice sheet still moved continuously, we positioned the rudder amidships and then locked the wheel with its mechanical brake so that it would not be exposed to more stress and strain than necessary. As soon as the ice became so thick that both the boat and the ice sat perfectly stationary, we loosened the brake again so as to not overload the wires. But, apparently, there was still too much tension.

To put an end to the banging, I get up, dress again, switch on the deck lights, and crawl out to the aft deck. I tie a rope around the tiller and secure each end to a bollard. I leave some slack in the rope. Were there no play, the tiller would bend when the boat gets knocked over. I wonder about the rudder, but I won't be able to determine if anything has happened to it until this wind moderates.

The following morning there's a message in our electronic mailbox from Jim, the winter radio operator at Palmer Station, informing us that their biggest antenna was knocked down by the 80-knot wind they measured last night. Our estimation of the wind speed here must have been right; Palmer is nowhere near as exposed as we are in this wind direction.

When it gets light, we go out to inspect the extent of the damage. The paint has sustained two small scratches just above the waterline, but there is nary a dent in the hull. Unbelievable! It's still quite windy, and each time the boat heels, we watch the steel plates scrape against the ice, but the rounded hull never gets stuck. Any hard-chine boat, or one with more flared topsides, would certainly have been damaged. The part of the rudder visible above the snow is neither twisted nor bent. To inspect the rudder itself, we dig up the ice around the stern. The ice is two feet (half a metre) thick and the digging takes a couple of hours, but then we see that the rudder has not been damaged either. What a relief.

Still, we don't want to expose the rudder to any risk for the rest of the winter. We dig until it can swing freely in both directions. We let the pool freeze overnight and then shovel loose snow on top of the newly formed ice cover. As long as the snow insulates as we expect it to, we figure that to keep the rudder safe we'll only have to remove a half a foot of ice each fortnight from now on.

MIKE STROUD

# SHADOWS ON THE WASTELAND

**T**HEN THINGS changed.

For the first time since entering the glacier system, the icy blast from the plateau decreased to the extent that it became manageable for sailing. It wasn't blowing straight down the glacier, and if we sailed, it would carry us in towards Wedge Face, but we couldn't resist a chance to move a few miles at less dreadful cost. Wedge Face was still more than ten miles distant and, knowing our luck, we would get no more than a short ride. Then we could angle out again to pass the crevasse field. Even if the wind continued, the mountain itself might turn it, allowing us to sail outwards again.

We got out the chutes and moved off. Here on the smooth soft snow, with no sastrugi, it was all so much easier than it had been the couple of times before. We raced along, the skis swishing through two inches of shimmering crystals, only the ski-tips showing as they hissed through the soft white blanket. We were exhilarated, and caution was literally thrown to the wind as the black cliff of Wedge Face drew nearer. Finally, instead of dying, the wind became too strong and we had to stop for our own safety, but we had been blown along for more than an hour, and had saved nearly a whole day's travel. We were thrilled, but not for long.

By the time we had put the chutes away visibility had become very limited. Loose snow was being driven along the surface, obscuring everything up to a height of about ten feet. Above, the sky was a deep blue, and the mountain peaks on the far side of the glacier gleamed in low orange sunlight, topped by nacreous clouds. Towering over us, blotting out a whole quadrant of the sky, rose the massive bulk of the darkly shadowed hanging cliff of Wedge Face. We started walking south-west with a view to rounding the mountain and, we hoped, the crevasse field as well. The wind was at least force ten and the spindrift swept and swirled around us, hissing along and hiding the ground ahead.

Suddenly we both saw it, right in our path. There, rising out of the blowing mist, was an enormous hump-back of fragmented, disrupted and tortuous ice. It must have risen to a hundred feet and extended away to our left as far as we could see. We stopped and looked, wondering what to do. Either we had to make a massive diversion to avoid it or we took it on direct. It would be slow to cross, but the direct approach must save time. We plumped for the frontal assault and began to climb.

The slope rose steadily, broken by huge cracks, most of them running across our path and the line of the slope. This was to be expected, and by zig-zagging back and forth, we could find the places where the gaps narrowed and were bridged by snow. Slowly we climbed towards the middle of the disturbance. As we crossed the convexity we came to a region of total anarchy. The ice was split in all directions and it seemed as if more of the area was occupied by black voids than by white surface. Furthermore, most of the surface consisted of the wind-blasted blue glass, with just a few patches of soft snow which formed into crevasse bridges. It made things very difficult. It would have been suicidal to cross the bridges without skis, yet elsewhere they skittered sideways on the glassy surfaces which funnelled towards the deep canyons. Worse, the sledges had a mind of their own, slewing sideways at the least opportunity and doing their best to drag us to destruction. It was terrifying. At any time it seemed as if one could slip, fall or be pulled over, and nothing would have stopped one from disappearing through the gaping mouths, down into the dark black throats.

We made our way through like men in a maze, wandering back and forth, seeking bridges strong enough to bear us, and turning aside from chasms too large to cross. Our course meandered so much, and it would have been so cold if we delayed, that neither of us suggested using a rope. We just took our chances and looked for the routes that seemed strong. We both moved as fast as we could but Ran was once again hurrying, taking advantage of his height to heave his sledge up, down and round the obstacles. I followed more slowly, my ankle complaining bitterly at these new found inclines. I was back at a disadvantage and was not impressed by the return of intolerant glares and beckonings. Still, I was not quite so demoralised at being left behind and was indeed grateful to be there. At least everything I crossed Ran had crossed first, and with him being the heavier man, I thought I had a good chance of survival.

After almost four hours, in which we moved less than a mile, we began to descend slowly through a second area of simple transverse cracks to reach the flat ice on the other side. We had made it through. With the wind dying, the visibility improved and we could look to the north. Ahead, the huge river now seemed to be quite smooth, rolling only gently as it forged a last straight slash through the mountains. Far away to the right there was an unmistakable silhouette. Neither of us had ever seen it before but we both knew what it was. Rising vertically from the ice, a six-thousand-foot wall of red granite towered to a pointed summit. It was a peak out of Gormenghast, as unreal as a child's drawing. It was Mount Kyffin, the finger. Along with Mount Hope on the opposite side of the Beardmore Glacier, it pointed to the end of what was probably the final stage of our journey – the far side of the continent.

We camped that night beyond the crevasses. At the foot of the Wedge Face. Ensconced once more in our tiny shelter, we reviewed our situation.

'We've got nine and a half rations left,' I said. 'That's nineteen days if we leave no reserve at all. How long did Messner take from here?'

'About nineteen,' Ran replied, 'mainly sailing, but with some quite big hauling days. We could do it if we have the wind.'

'Maybe,' I responded, 'but only if we get more than he did. We're in no shape to make any big pulls, and there's also your feet. I don't suppose they would last.'

'It would have to be a raging infection to stop us getting to the main goal,' laughed Ran. 'I'm not intending to give up now.'

That was fair enough. We had come about thirteen hundred miles as the crow flies, and probably fifteen hundred in reality. To complete a crossing of the continent there were only thirty or so to go, but I wasn't sure that that was the main goal.

'And beyond the Gate?' I asked.

'That's more difficult,' he said, 'but I want to make the ice shelf so, while there's still a chance, I think we should go for it. As long as you're ready to stop when the chance slips away.'

'That's fine by me,' I said. 'I realise that getting to Scott Base is pretty unlikely and I guess we'll just have to settle for the continent.'

'Well, don't sound so down about it,' Ran chided me. 'It's not a failure. We will have achieved something remarkable. I never reckoned we'd get anywhere near this far.'

'So why did you do it?' I asked. 'If you thought it was impossible, like I did, it couldn't have been for the money – that awful answer you give the press.'

'Yes, I suppose that's true,' he said thoughtfully. 'I'm not sure really, though money must be a big part of it because I wouldn't do it if it weren't my career.'

'Ah, but you chose your career, it didn't choose you,' I responded. 'You made it your living because you were good at the outdoor sort of things – winning biathlons, canoe instructor and all that. Because you were good at them, you enjoyed them, or perhaps vice versa. You must get some pleasure from these journeys.'

'I suppose I do,' he said quietly. 'Although this one has been pretty nasty. I'll admit that I enjoy talking about them afterwards, and I'm pleased to share them with the people that read the books or hear me speak. I'm also pleased that this will be a British success, but I won't start talking about the view or the philosophical stuff because, if I do, I'll be labelled a woolly-minded eccentric aristocrat. I'd rather the press said I was mercenary. At least everyone can relate to that.'

'Well, I think I'll relate to the woolly bits.' I smiled. 'And anyway, I thought you were French.'

Only one more obstacle lay between us and the completion of the crossing. Where the Beardmore flowed into the Ross ice shelf, there would be another region of ice disruption, though there was a way past this one. When Shackleton pioneered the way south in 1908, and discovered the Beardmore, he found a safe entrance to the bottom end, the route he called 'the Gate'. It was a clever jink, taking the traveller behind Mount Hope and allowing him to slip past the area of major crevassing by using two minor valleys linked by a narrow col. All expeditions since have followed his path, and now we just had to reach that gateway, which we knew was marked by the Granite Towers.

On the following morning we set off. The sun was shining and the air was completely still. It was cold, about minus 40° C. The snow was sticky and the sledge heavy, and my back ached, but I felt renewed. To reach the Gate would be a triumph. Keep going and we would have done something special. Mount Kyffin helped. It grew larger and more glorious by the hour – a vertical marker at the peak of our horizontal mountain. The sight lifted me and my mind now pushed my feeble body. For the first time since before the mountains, I found the going easier than Ran. He had slowed, for even the end of the tunnel could not relieve the pain that rose to dominate his mind. He was hobbled and miserable, and I feared that the infection was finally taking off. But we made our requisite distance, and that night camped again, with less than twenty miles to go. It had been our ninetieth day of travel. Surely nothing could stop us now.

The next day, after a few hours' hauling, the air stirred once more. Then our hoods began to rustle as the white crystals kicked up by our skis started to flee before us. The wind became stronger, but it was intermittent and we went on hauling, thinking of the gusts as there to mock us. But they persisted. We opened our sails and were finally carried steadily forward, borne on the wind that for half our journey had been an enemy and for most of the rest an absent ally. It carried us the extra miles and soon, across the broadening frozen delta, we saw the Granite Towers and the entrance to our road. Suddenly it looked as if we could make it that day. We pressed on, not stopping for our tepid soup. As we drew closer, the Towers became greater, and what had appeared an ordinary broken cliff grew into huge red-granite pillars – a temple made for giants, a gateway to release.

There was a crevassed region at the foot of the Towers, where we had to stop sailing and move carefully. Slowly we crossed these last few mantraps, and as we did so, the monoliths slipped aside, and there before us lay our path. There were just a few hours more to go.

We approached the col together. It was so late in our evening that the sun was in the north, and we came up in deep shadow. Ahead, through the narrow saddle the sky was ablaze, and as we climbed those last few yards the grey unlit snow ignited round our feet. We reached the divide and stood in silence. Behind us the dark valley of our journey, three months of mental and physical hell, before us a sunlit world of freedom. A snow-covered slope, flanked by screes, dropped steeply to merge with the ice shelf in another region of cracks. Further out there were more local disturbances but the eye didn't rest there. It was the world beyond that drew our gaze. The whole vastness of the Ross ice shelf lay in front of us, stretching east, west, and north to the horizon. We had completed our journey. Whether we stopped here or carried on, this was the place that would mark our accomplishment. Here, and at that moment, we had reached the shore of the Pacific Ocean.

Ran smiled. I pushed back the tears. We shook hands.

'You owe me a meal at Simpson's,' I said.

# NORTH AMERICA

## GRAHAM MACKINTOSH

# INTO A DESERT PLACE
## A 3000 Mile Walk around
## the Coast of Baja California

**T**HE FISHING was steadily improving as I headed south. Fish, shellfish, seaweed and cactus, there was certainly food in abundance. But one never knows what Baja will dish up next.

One morning, I was searching for something to eat when I came across a seal pup. He was high and dry and all alone, looking up at me with his big innocent eyes. I was so hungry, all I could see was forty pounds of seal meat roasting on a stick. Fingering my machete, I looked guiltily around. I should have hit him hard, quick and clean. Instead, I kept staring at those eyes. They seemed to be saying, 'Are you my daddy?' I thought of all the Seaworld seals I'd seen and I couldn't do it; or rather I wasn't quite desperate enough. I reached forward to pat him on his chestnut-brown head. He rose up hissing and honking and showing his Alsatian-like teeth. I didn't think the beach was the safest place for him. So, using a bit of gentle encouragement from my boot, I manoeuvred him back into the sea and carried on with a good conscience and an empty belly.

A little while later, the low tide invited me to find my lunch in the pools and crevices of a rocky platform reaching well out to sea. It was there that I first made the acquaintance of the abalone – a large limpet-like shellfish that grows as big as a breakfast bowl. They cling to the smooth rocks with a powerful muscular 'foot'. Once they pull the shell down tight, it's almost impossible to get them off. Speed and surprise are what counts. I learned to thrust the blade of my machete under the shell and lever them off before they sensed what was happening.

The ear-shaped shell has a characteristic line of holes along one edge. Inside, it is a beautiful blue-grey, iridescent, mother of pearl. Even more beautiful to me was the sight of the large, muscular foot. After a few minutes boiling, the creature easily came away from its shell, and a quick pull separated the meaty foot from the innards. It was as delicious as a piece of prime steak.

One day, with just two pints of water left, my mouth dry and my throat parched, exhilaration and excitement reverted once again to apprehension and fear. I began preparing myself for the ordeal ahead. The falling tide enabled me to walk on a narrow stretch of fine-gravel beach beneath a line of low, yellow cliffs. I stepped over yet another rivulet of water draining back to the sea. 'Strange!' I thought. 'Where's all that coming from?' It couldn't have been left by the tide. I walked back, scooped up a handful and tasted it. It was fresh! Fresh water, coming from a spring at the base of the cliffs. Hardly able to believe my luck, I threw down my pack, made a fire, filled the kettle and sat drinking cup after cup of coffee. I dug a hole in the beach and diverted the trickle of water into it. The fresh water pool that formed was perfect for washing myself and my clothes. Water! What marvellous stuff it was. I left a gallon of it warming inside one of the chlorine bottles, then I enjoyed the sheer sensual delight of pouring it slowly over my head. With hardly a care in the world, I relived my water-loving childhood as I wandered among the rockpools playing with the crabs and the anemones, and looking for lunch. With an unlimited supply of fresh water I could eat as much as I wanted. It was a terrific feeling.

About 5 p.m., however, the rising tide forced me to leave. Struggling with the weight of three gallons of water, I was able to cover another four miles before dark. I made camp in a little side canyon cut into the cliffs, and slept well. Three gallons of water meant another three days walking and another thirty miles closer to Guerrero Negro.

A fishcamp saved me from the next water crisis. Gone was the 'don't drink the water' and 'get out of camp before dark' mentality. Usually I couldn't wait to get in!

The camp was situated on an arc of beach in a beautiful, sheltered south-facing bay. There was an abnormal amount of mid-day activity, for most of the fishermen had just arrived for the opening of the lobster season. I was offered a cup of coffee and a place to sleep in a little shack bashed together against a wall of sand and gravel. It wouldn't have looked too out-of-place in a trench on the Somme.

I preferred to put my tent higher up overlooking the Pacific. The coast ahead was intimidating. A great rounded block of mountain fell precipitously down to the water. I was in the mood for enjoying myself while I could, and was helped by the arrival of a group of middle-aged Americans who'd braved the thirty-mile drive in from the main highway. They were surprised to see me. One of them, looking up and down the coast, said, 'You've certainly got balls,' in a way suggesting that he didn't think I'd have them much longer.

Promising a 'special treat', they invited me to join them for dinner. One of them had bought a sack of lobster from the fishermen. I'd never eaten lobster before and I was quickly disillusioned about how to prepare them. I had always assumed that you simply drop them into boiling water. Instead, one of the Americans pulled a bewildered-looking specimen from the sack. Holding it down on a block of wood, he took a heavy knife and cut off the twelve-inch-long feelers at the front. Then he chopped away the wriggling legs down one side, and then down the other. The poor creature hardly had time to come to terms with this loss before he said goodbye to his tail, got a knife in his back, and was cut down the middle, smeared with butter and popped on a grill.

With the remains of the lobster twitching and sizzling away, we all stood around the fire, pouring drinks, swapping stories and reflecting on how wonderful life can be. I didn't think it was quite so wonderful when I was given the knife and a particularly lively lobster, and invited to prepare my own dinner.

I held the strange beast as if it was a creature from outer space. The Pacific lobster, unlike the more familiar Maine lobster, has no claws. It relies on its tough, spiny shell and its snappy, sharp-edged tail for defence.

'Watch your hand!' someone shouted.

Just in time, I shifted my grip as the tail snapped viciously. As I chopped and stabbed away, I had no idea that this 'special treat' was about to become a very familiar part of my diet.

The following morning, I wrote some letters and gave them to the Americans to post. They gave me a stock of chocolate chip cookies, candy bars, oranges and all the water I could carry. Some of the Mexicans gave me a bag of tortillas and a detailed account of what lay ahead. If I could get beyond a bad stretch of about four miles of cliffs I would find several miles of 'easy' walking – low bluffs, rounded hills and sandy beaches. They warned me to keep an eye open for a wild and savage white-tailed coyote with a reputation for attacking people.

After waiting for the tide to start falling, I strapped my machete to my belt, picked up my heavy load and walked off towards the daunting line of cliffs. I was able to walk several hundred yards in the desert before being forced down on to the stony beach. It was very difficult walking. The beach dropped steeply into the sea. I was sliding down so much with the pebbles, it was like continually walking uphill. And any flat stretches tended to be covered with an awkward tangle of driftwood, bones and barrels.

At least on the rocks under the cliffs, I was able to make faster, less exhausting, progress. But then I started falling. I dented the kettle; I banged my knee; I landed on top of one of the water containers, splitting it wide open and losing over two pints of water; and last, but not least, I dashed my shin against a sharp rock leaving behind a not very pretty mix of skin, hair and blood. Luckily, I was able to hobble on. Being on rocks beneath cliffs with the tide rising was a great anaesthetic.

Working my way around the final barrier of rock before the promised stretch of beach, I surprised a pack of a dozen or more coyotes feasting on a dead seal. I whipped out my machete as they scattered in every direction. One was having his after-dinner nap and didn't realise he'd been deserted by his buddies till I stood over him and coughed politely. I don't think he stopped running till he got to Cabo!

A few days later, I was following a coyote trail along a particularly difficult bit of coast. In spite of the trail, it was slow, painful progress, a dangerous series of ups and downs on loose, crumbling rock. I had just two pints of water, and was sweating and drinking continuously.

At one point – where the trail ran along a short, boulder-strewn stretch of stony beach – I found a washed-up lobster trap. There was a large lobster still alive inside! No point leaving him there to die in the sun. I popped him in a plastic bag and looked forward to a lobster dinner.

The coyote trail led me up on to a ledge sandwiched between a sheer wall of red rock rising to vulture-circling heights on my left and a line of sheer cliffs falling away to the gulls gliding two hundred feet below. The ledge seemed to be narrowing all the time. Yet I pushed on. Coyote trails always went somewhere.

The trail wound confidently and purposefully along the ledge. If I lost it, I'd circle and zigzag till I picked it up again. The trail was a guide and a friend, a laid-down direction that kept at bay that chilling sense of being lost and alone.

The unscaleable slope above came closer and closer to joining that below. The trail just ended. It had to. The wall of rock fell almost sheer from the mountain peak to the sea. Not even a coyote could get by. I sat down and tried to come to terms with adding the pain of retreat to the unpleasantnesses of fear, thirst and uncertainty.

A mile back down the trail, I was faced with a dilemma. I could either go all the way down to the rocks and try to make my way under the cliffs, or I could climb a ridge to the top of the mountain and try to find a way down the other side.

As the climb down to the shore looked too dangerous, I decided to go up. After an hour I made it, legs trembling, to the peak. The view was spectacular. As if he were anxious to have a look, the lobster started wriggling around in the bag and, in a moment of frivolity, I held the curious crustacean aloft to give him a glimpse of life at 2,000 feet. But my mood turned a little more serious as I searched for the best way down. Apart from leaping off, the only certain way was the way I'd come up. The backside of the mountain had just fallen away into nothing. In spite of my exhaustion, fear gave me the strength to backtrack down the ridge and climb down to the water. I was certainly seeing Baja from every angle.

With renewed optimism I pushed on beneath the cliffs. The waves of crystal-clear water rolled in, exploding against the rocks. With water rushing and cascading all around, it was a hopeless task trying to keep my feet dry, so I put on my tennis shoes and tied my boots around my neck. Learning from the many crabs dashing and clinging, dashing and clinging, I edged along the base of the cliffs, throwing myself at the wall and holding tight as the worst of the waves threatened.

After half an hour I was beginning to think that I might make it past that awkward mountain when I came across a deep channel of water surging into a cave in the cliffs. Shit! There was no way over; and there'd be no help from the tide. It was already at its lowest.

I stood staring at the limpet-studded wall of rock on the other side of the channel. Ten feet away! It might as well have been ten miles. Inside, I was a boiling mix of disappointment, anxiety, frustration and anger. The tide would soon be rising. I had to get out from under those cliffs quick.

I made my way back along the rocks, and climbed up to the coyote trail. The retreat continued. I abandoned all thoughts of making progress. Desperately thirsty, the only thing that mattered now was water. I followed the trail back for two miles looking for a suitable beach to set up my stills. The narrow sandy floor at the mouth of a steep-sided canyon was perfect. There was no time to lose. I swallowed my last mouthful of water and pulled out my stills. It was too late in the day to get much from the solar still. For the first time, I would have to boil seawater. Looking at the cheap, battered aluminium kettle and the flimsy plastic tubing, I felt a rush of panic. Supposing it didn't work? Supposing I'd damaged the kettle in one of those falls? Supposing the tubing melted or my matches were wet?

With my life on the line, I looked back in disbelief at the cavalier way I'd tested the kettle-still in Los Angeles. I had played with it for fifteen minutes, got a little drinkable water, and jumped around in naïve satisfaction. Someone should have banged me on the head, to remind me of what I'd read in the survival literature: 'fear, panic and distress can kill in hours' . . . 'How many castaways through the ages have become stiff and sudden corpses, killed, not by the sea, not by hunger or thirst, but by their own terror?' . . . 'The cure for panic is a thorough knowledge of your survival equipment and the confidence that this brings.'

So much had gone wrong that day, it was hard to imagine anything going right. I clambered over the dam-like barrier of pebbles that had been dumped across the mouth of the valley. The stones dropped steeply into the sea; so steep there was hardly any surf, just a powerful rise and fall of water. Standing knee deep, I immersed the kettle and a water container. The bubbles rose for a few seconds, then the sea dropped, leaving me surrounded by tumbling pebbles. When the sea rushed back, it rose in a great explosive surge that lifted me off my feet and carried me away. The kettle was torn from my hand. I watched in horror as it slowly sank in the foam before me. Releasing the water container, I sent both hands slapping and slicing through the sea till I got hold of the handle and held on for dear life. I was also able to grab back the water-bottle before kicking furiously towards the beach. The sea several times pushed me to within touching distance, then raked me back like a cat playing with a mouse. Eventually, I got my feet down and, running faster than the pebbles were tumbling, scrambled up to safety.

The experience didn't do much for my nerves, and swallowing a mouthful of seawater didn't do much for my thirst. Shaking deep down, if not visibly, I went off in search of a rock pool.

I quickly got the fire going, then put the kettle on to boil. As the steam came blowing through the plastic tube, I passed it into my aluminium water bottle which soon became 'boiling hot'. Most of the steam was rising and escaping, so I placed the water bottle in a saucepan of cold seawater. Every minute I shook it to see how much water had condensed inside. At last, I seemed to be getting something. I poured a mouthful into my cup. Ugh! It was salty. My life depended on it being fresh and it was salty. Trying to stay calm, I threw away the yield and tried again.

For ten thirst-tortured, nail-biting minutes, I waited for more water to condense. It was still salty. Why? Steam is pure water. Where was the salt coming from?

Panic and dehydration were wringing my brain for a drop of water. I couldn't think straight. In a moment of madness, I almost kicked the still across the beach. I shut my eyes and clenched my fists as I struggled to compose myself. Remember, 'killed not by hunger or thirst but by their own terror'. Suddenly the sergeant was back beside me, not shouting and bawling but calm and reassuring: 'Come on. It'll work. Let's try again.' I looked up into the sunset and just for a second I thought I saw him in his scarlet tunic. My mind was playing tricks, but it was the distraction I needed.

I picked up the still. All I could think of was, maybe the kettle was too full; maybe boiling water was being carried through with the steam? I poured out half the seawater, and put the kettle back on the fire with the spout end raised a bit.

I scalded my lips in my anxiety to test the next batch. I didn't care. I could have drunk a gallon of it. It was fresh, beautiful, life-sustaining, brain-clearing, fresh water. Having got things sorted out, I began producing water at the rate of a cup an hour.

Unable to sit still, I left the kettle simmering on a low fire and went, machete in hand, to explore the little canyon. After a hundred yards it opened out. The sheer walls gave way to rounded yellow hills. Apart from the very few desiccated bushes and cacti, the dusty, washed-out slopes wouldn't have looked out of place on the moon. Further inland the mountains looked mauve in the evening light.

The floor of the valley was sterile sand, easy walking. It seemed the obvious route into the mountains and hopefully around the impasse on the coast. I wandered up one of the slopes looking for a barrel cactus, and found one a bit bigger than I would have liked; but there was no point worrying about conservation now. I managed to unearth the cactus and carry it by its roots back to the camp. I almost ran. I couldn't shake off the feeling of anxiety. Supposing a coyote was running off with my still, supposing the plastic tubing had caught fire? You name it, I saw it happening.

Having slaked my thirst, I allowed myself to think of food. I had as much barrel cactus as I could eat, but lobster was beginning to sound very tempting. Before dispatching the strange looking beast, I studied him carefully. With his armour plating, jointed appendages and spiny back he didn't look nearly as good as he tasted. I hated the idea of chopping him up or dropping him in boiling water, so I resorted to another method I'd seen the Mexicans use – I grabbed his tail, bent it over, then twisted and pulled. All his armour made no difference. There was a horrible cracking sound as the lobster broke in two. I'm not sure if it was any more humane, but once I'd thrown the head end in the sea, I was left with a hunk of meat in my hand. I cut it down the middle, pulled out the string of gut, then dropped both sides into a pan of boiling seawater. Lobster followed by barrel cactus, followed by coffee, satisfied my hunger and my thirst.

I sat by the fire tending the still until the early hours of the morning. When I'd made about two and a half pints of water, I felt relaxed enough to crawl into the tent and get some sleep. A coyote sent up a chilling howl from deep in the valley. Perhaps it was White Tail. I slipped the machete beneath my pillow and stared up at the stars through the tent. My heavy eyelids flickered, then brought down the curtain on a day I wanted to forget.

PICO IYER

# FALLING OFF THE MAP
## Some Lonely Places of the World

D RIVING ALONG the one-lane roads, past sunlit fields of sugar-
cane, we pass billboards honouring the great revolutionary
heroes (Martí, Guevara, O'Higgins), signs declaring SPEED IS THE
ALLY OF DEATH, lonely ceiba trees and goat-drawn carts. Flying
Pigeon bicycles are everywhere, and vintage Plymouths, and hissing, rusted buses. Sometimes we stop to pick up hitchhikers, and
Louis serenades them with passages from *The Waste Land*, ditties
from the Grateful Dead, and – his latest attraction – manically pan-
tomimed scenes from *The Jerk*. Bicycles, chickens, children swarm
and swerve across the roads. I remember the time in Morocco
when, on our way to the airport, he hit a dog. The dog bounded off
unhindered; our Citroën limped to a halt.

Then, suddenly, out of nowhere, a bicycle swerves in front of
us, there is a sickening thud, and our windshield shatters, splattering us with glass. I cannot bear to get out to see what has happened. But somehow, miraculously, the boy on the bicycle has
been thrown out of the path of the car and gets up, only shaken.

A crowd forms, and, a few minutes later, a policeman appears.

'We're so sorry,' I tell him. 'If there's anything we can do . . .'

'No problem,' he says, patting me on the shoulder. 'Don't
worry. These things happen. We're sorry if this has spoiled your
holiday in Cuba.'

Spoiled our holiday? We've almost spoiled the poor boy's life!

'Don't worry,' he assures me with a smile. 'There is just some
paperwork. Then you can go on.'

116

A car comes up, and two more imposing cops get out. They take some notes, then barrel up towards us. 'These boys,' says one. 'No, no. It was entirely our fault.' 'These young boys,' he goes on. 'You will just have to fill out some forms, and then you can be on your way.'

Soon we are taken to a hospital, where a young nurse hits me on the wrist. Then she asks me to extend my arms, to touch my nose, to touch my nose with my eyes closed. Luckily, it is a big target: I pass with flying colours.

Then we are taken to the local police station, a bare, pink-walled shack in the town's main plaza. Inside, a few locals are diligently observing a solitary sign which requests them to SPEAK IN A LOUD VOICE.

Across from us sits our hapless victim, next to a middle-aged man. Sizing up the situation, we go over to him. 'Look, we can't apologise enough for what we did to your son. It was all our fault. If there is any . . .'

'No, no, my friends.' He smiles. 'Is nothing. Please enjoy your time in Cuba.' Louis, overwhelmed, presents the family with a box of Dundee Shortbread, purchased, for just such occasions, at the Heathrow Duty-Free Lounge. A festive air breaks out.

Then we are ushered into an inner office. A black man motions me to sit before his desk and hand him my passport. 'So, Señor Pico.' 'My surname, actually, is Iyer.' 'So your father's name is Pico.' 'No, my father's name is Iyer.' 'But here it says Iyer, Pico.' 'Yes. My family's name is Iyer.' 'So your mother's name is Pico.' 'No. My father's name is Iyer.' 'So your mother's name is . . .' This goes on for a while, and then a baby-faced cop with an Irish look comes in. He claps a hand on Louis's shoulder. Where are we from? England. 'No wonder he looks like Margaret Thatcher,' he exclaims, and there is more jollity all around. Then he leans forward again. 'But you are from India, no?' Yes. 'Then tell me something.' His face is all earnest inquiry. 'Rajiv Gandhi is the son of Indira Gandhi?' Yes. 'And the grandson of the other Gandhi?' 'No. He is the grandson of Nehru. No relation to the other Gandhi.' 'No relation, eh? Not a grandson of the other

Gandhi?' The Irishman shakes his head in wonder, and the black man sits back to take this thunderbolt in. Then he resumes typing out his report six times over, without benefit of carbons.

Finally, he turns to Louis. 'So your family name is Louis,' he begins. 'No, no,' I break in, and add, 'he cannot speak Spanish.' There is a hasty consultation. Then the Irishman pads off, only to return a few minutes later with a trim, round-faced boss with glasses and a tie. *'Guten Tag,'* cries the police chief, extending a hand toward me. 'No, no,' I say. 'It's him.' The police chief spins around. *'Guten Tag,'* he cries, greeting Louis like a long-lost friend and proceeding to reminisce about a *'Freundin'* he once knew in Leipzig. Things are going swimmingly now. 'Margaret Thatcher, very sexy woman!' exclaims the Irishman. 'Rajiv Gandhi is not the grandson of the other Gandhi,' explains the black man to a newcomer. *'Aber, diese Mädchen . . .'* the police chief reminisces. We could almost be at a Christmas dinner, so full of smiles and clapped shoulders is the room. 'If this were anywhere else,' Louis whispers, 'if this were England, in fact, and a foreigner hit a local boy, they'd probably be lynching him by now.'

At six o'clock – it is clear that the police plan to make a day of it – the police chief invites us to dinner at the town's only hotel. Guests of the police, he says. We sit down, and Louis spots a glass of beer. He orders one, and drinks it. Then another. Then another. The chief orders more beers all round, then proposes a toast to *Die Freundschaft*. The waitress drops off a few beers. 'She worked in Czechoslovakia for four years,' the chief proudly informs us. 'How is the weather now in Prague?' Louis asks her in Czech. 'I worked for four years in a Trabant factory,' she answers. The police chief, exultant, proposes more toasts to *Die Freundschaft*.

'Paraguay is the only place in the world where you win at blackjack even if you're only even with the bank,' offers Louis.

*'Gut, gut, sehr gut!'* cries the chief, more animated than ever.

We renew a few pledges to eternal friendship, then get up and return to the police station, which is sleepy now in the dark.

Louis sits down and promptly slumps over. A group of policemen gathers round him to peer at his handless watch.

Then, suddenly, he sits up. 'I'm feeling really terrible,' he announces and, lurching out to the terrace, proceeds to deposit some toasts to *Die Freundschaft* in the bushes.

The police chief, anxious, comes over. 'I'm sorry,' I explain. 'We haven't eaten properly for a few days, we were somewhat dehydrated already, and he's probably anyway in a state of shock.' With a look of infinite tenderness, the chief summons a lieutenant, and, one on either side of Louis, they take him to the hospital.

Ten minutes later, the team returns, all smiles.

'How are you feeling?'

'Great. All better now.'

'Good.'

Louis slumps over again, and I maintain our vigil for the man from the car rental firm who is due to take us to Santiago. He was expected at two-thirty. It is now nine-fifteen.

Suddenly, a policeman walks into the room and summons me urgently over. I hurry to his side. Maybe he will give us a lift? 'You are an Indian?' he says.

'Yes.'

'Then tell me something.' He points to a TV. 'Two months ago, we saw Rajiv Gandhi being burned. Why did they not put his body in the ground?'

What is the Spanish word for 'cremation'? I wonder wildly. *'Cremación,'* I try.

'Cremation, eh? Is that right? Thank you,' he says, and walks out.

A little later, Louis gets up again and staggers to the terrace. More toasts to *Die Freundschaft* go down the drain.

'I'm really sick,' he says. 'I can't move. Just get me a bed.'

I relay the request to the police chief.

For the first time all day, his commitment to our friendship seems to flag. *'Hier gibt es kein Bett!'* he barks. *'Das ist nicht Hotel! Das ist nicht Krankenhaus!'*

*'Jawohl, mein Herr,'* I say, and we go on waiting for the car rental man.

Suddenly, headlights sweep into the plaza, and a car pulls up. I hurry outside. A man gets out, with an air of great briskness, and

I hurry over to him. 'So you are Indian?' he says. 'Yes.' 'Then tell me something, please. When Rajiv Gandhi died, why did they not put his body in the ground?'

'Cremation,' I reply with tired fluency, and, satisfied, he gets in his car and drives away.

Watching this open-air university in action, the police chief is shamed, perhaps, by his earlier brusqueness. 'Once,' he tells me in German, 'I travelled for six hours by train to Dresden to meet my roommate's sister.'

'Ach ja?'

At 11.15 pm, the car rental man appears, and we return to the inner office to do some paperwork. 'So – your name is Pico?' 'Well, my family name is Iyer.' 'So your father's name is Pico.' 'No . . .'

At 1.15 am, we pull up at last in front of the Casagranda Hotel in Santiago ('simultaneously dirty and suffocating', sings my guidebook), a famous old joint recently closed for fumigation, where we have a four-day reservation, paid for in advance in London. I leave Louis comatose in the back of our new car, sundry revellers singing and banging drums around him in the street. Inside the hotel, an enormous man is sitting next to a wooden cash register. When he sees my voucher, he looks unhappy. Party girls in backless dresses and well-coiffed boys stroll down the pitch-black staircase from the rooftop cabaret. A couple of them sit on a couch in the lobby and gaze expectantly in my direction. The enormous man looks desperate. I look worse. He picks up a telephone and starts dialling.

Thirty minutes later, he has found us alternative accommodations. At 2.15 am., a convoy of two cars, including one spokesman for the house of Gandhi, one new rental car and one immobile investment banker, pulls up at the Hotel Gaviota. As soon as it does, a young boy rushes out. 'Welcome,' he cries, in English. 'How was your trip? Welcome to the Hotel Gaviota! It's great to see you!'

'Thanks.'

'We have some Welcome Cocktails all ready for you! What will it be? A cuba libre? A daiquiri? Some *ron*? What would you like?'

'My friend cannot move.'

'No problem. A Welcome Cocktail will help. It's on the house!'

'But he's already heard Margaret Thatcher impugned, almost killed a boy, and been taken to a hospital by a police chief speaking German.'

'Sure!' says the boy. 'That's why he needs a Welcome Cocktail. Please! My friends are waiting!' He points to the bar, where two young bloods are sitting hopefully in the dark.

I go over to Louis, now propped up in the lobby, and break the news to him.

He does not look overjoyed.

'The thing is, unless you order a Welcome Cocktail, I don't think you'll get a room.'

'OK, OK, just get me some mineral water.' Realising that this could entail a long wait – yesterday we had stopped in a small town to ask two boys for water and been told, 'For water you must go to the next town! Only forty-five kilometres away!' – I go to the desk to do some paperwork. On one side is a sign that advises, CRAZY LOVE IS NOT TRUE LOVE. On the other, a stack of Cubatur brochures. *'Ven a vivir una tentación!'* Come to live out a temptation!

Proprieties observed, we follow our host on the ten-minute walk to our suites, made-for-mobster caverns from the fifties, with mirrors all round, and enormous makeup areas for showgirls.

'This is OK?' the young boy asks.

'Sure,' I say. But one thing still bothers me: why doesn't he care about the fate of Rajiv Gandhi?

# TED CONOVER

# ROLLING NOWHERE

**T**HE SUN HAD FALLEN to the point where its hot rays streamed directly through the boxcar doorway, coaxing me from the shade, when the train rolled slowly into a long, dusty yard and squealed to a stop. *Whooooosh* – I heard the noise that means the same thing to hoboes as the airline stewardess's "We have arrived at the gate . . ." I dropped out the doorway into the hot Indian-summer afternoon. Moments later, the black man I had seen a few hours before did the same. I nodded in his direction, and presently he lifted a hand and waved at me. Slowly, casually, we approached each other. Then I committed my first faux pas: I offered my hand.

He looked at it strangely; his right arm seemed to twitch, but did not immediately rise. "How you doin'?" we kind of said at the same time, and I did not drop my hand soon enough. Awkwardly, he lifted his and quickly we shook. Handshaking, I would learn after reflexively repeating my mistake two or three times with other hoboes, was a foreign mannerism here.

The man followed it by asking where I was headed.

"Oh, Lincoln, I guess," I replied.

"Yeah, I been thinkin' 'bout that too," he said, beginning to walk up the track. I fell into step with him. "Ain't nothin' goin' on here, y' know." Along with no handshake, I noticed, the man had not introduced himself. I held back on offering my name and glanced over at him as we walked.

He was wearing shiny black patent-leather shoes with no socks, dirty slacks, a buttondown short-sleeve shirt, and a soiled brown cap. He carried a water jug and a paper bag, which later I would learn contained some extra clothing. He was probably in his forties but looked younger. Very talkative, he was soon telling me how he had been surprised to see me catch the train "on the fly," as he put it, since "most guys just go into the yard, and climb on before it starts moving," as he had done in Kansas City. He stooped over to pick up a partly smoked cigarette someone had discarded.

"But don't they ever catch you?"

"Well, it all depends," he said. "Some lines are hot, like that Santa Fe, Union Pacific, Missouri Pacific – you don't see many tramps at all on them. Then you got the Burlington. They got – what do you call it – a humane attitude. Long as you stay sober, don't start no fires, don't get drunk, you can stay outa trouble on the Burlington."

Ah, so that's it, I thought: the reason why five days of railroading had yielded so few hoboes.

Our present location, he informed me, was St. Joseph, Missouri, on the far west side of the state. He had been here many times before; hoboes, he explained, pretty much had the run of this yard. The statement was borne out by people we met as we reached a road and began to cross the yard.

"Evenin', gents," said a conductor with an overnight bag waiting for his caboose. When my companion asked a brakeman where we could get water, he indicated we were welcome to go into the railroad workers' locker room and fill up at the sink.

Then I saw the hoboes. The first were a pair of old men, bearing their gear and walking slowly down one edge of the yard to a train that I had the momentary illusion was waiting for them. The next were an odd threesome – a gawky-looking guy about my age with a backpack and a belt buckle in the form of a marijuana leaf; a meek-looking, balding, dusty middle-aged man; and a fierce, explosive-seeming tramp with a deeply creased face, who confronted us as we neared the side of the yard.

"Hey!" he demanded of me. "Where's the Sally?"

"Who?" I asked, puzzled.

"Awww, shit." He nearly expectorated, disgusted that I didn't know what he was talking about, and too impatient to explain. But my companion understood.

"You find it about three miles up the tracks," he said. "Turn left when you see the stoplights."

"Three miles!" the old man snarled. "No way!" Turning to his companions, he said, "C'mon, let's go. These guys don't know what they're talkin' about." The young one objected, and nearly had his head taken off by the gruff old man. "You're either with me or you're not," he growled, striding off along the tracks. Reluctantly, the other two fell into file behind him.

On the side of the yard nearer St. Joseph the man and I found a grass patch to rest in and enjoy the end of the day. A "Sally," he explained to me, was tramp talk for a Salvation Army facility, just as "Willy" was a Goodwill Store, and "St. Vinnie's" was St. Vincent de Paul, a Catholic charity organization. Just before the sun set, I suggested that we walk into town to get groceries. He had some food stamps, he had confided, and I had a small amount of change in my pocket.

But he demurred, "Folks like me ain't welcome in this town till after dark," he said. He was probably referring to his black skin, but he may have meant his poor, train-dirtied clothing and the gear he carried, which identified him as a tramp.

"What about folks like me?" I asked.

The man shrugged. "You can try."

I headed up the sleepy, poor back streets in search of a grocery store. Finally I came upon one and, leaving my stuff outside, I bought milk, cheese, bread, sandwich meat, and a candy bar. Starving after the long train ride, I walked directly to a street corner and took a seat on my bedroll. I wasted no time in guzzling the quart of milk and making several sandwiches. I was so involved in eating that I barely noticed a dirty white pickup truck that slowed down as it turned my corner, and then parked just a few yards away.

The truck door opened. I nearly choked in mid-swallow when I looked up to see a huge overweight man lumber out of the driver's seat and plod toward me. Through the window of the cab, a puffy-faced woman I guessed was his wife was staring at me. The man's boots were heavy and his neck, exposed by a military-type haircut, was red.

Oh, no, I thought to myself as nausea swept over me. My first attack.

Trying to be casual, I slipped a hand down toward my pants pocket and the cartridge of Mace that rested there.

The man was walking directly toward me. I glanced again at the pickup. Fortunately, it had no rifle rack. There was a magnetic sign on the door. SAL BRODER, it said, ST. JOSEPH, MISSOURI. I would need that for the police report.

Sal Broder stopped just a few feet away. "Boy," he started, and I thought, here it comes. I noticed he had no teeth. "Boy, I know it ain't none of my business, but I just wanted to know how you're doin'. You broke?"

His words and tone were friendly – was it a ruse? Though I was still suspicious, a small wave of relief swept over me. I answered that I was on the road but no, I wasn't broke.

Sal Broder continued with a number of questions, interrupting himself to explain that he had left his teeth in the truck. "Are you sleeping on the ground?" he asked. "In jails? Did you run away from your parents? Where are you from?" Supposing in turn that I was not dangerous, Sal Broder sat down next to me on the curb. "Are you headed home?" I answered him as truthfully as possible without letting on about the hobo project, but he didn't really seem too concerned with the answers. He just wanted to express his concern.

"You know, I was a cop here when I was younger," he said. "Met a lot of young guys like you. Even took some home with me. Wife and I helped 'em get a fresh start. So when I saw you settin' there, you know what I said to her? I said, 'Honey, I'm going to give that boy a dollar.' " This Sal Broder proceeded to do, taking out his wallet and trying to put the dollar in my hand. But I resisted, insisting that I was not broke and that, though it was very kind of him to offer to help me out, I really was doing okay – and I showed him the food I just bought.

"Nonsense!" said Sal loudly, forcing the bill into my bedroll. "By the way, you ever been in trouble with the police?"

"No, never have."

"Well, keep it that way. If a policeman comes up to ya, tell him he's barkin' up the wrong tree."

A dollar poorer, Sal Broder then got back into his truck, said something to Mrs. Broder, and drove away. As what had happened became clear, I was filled with multiple emotions: incredulity, gratitude, shame for having suspected him, and a secret satisfaction that my mere appearance had prompted his generosity.

ALASTAIR SCOTT

# TRACKS ACROSS ALASKA
## A Dog Sled Journey

DURING MY two days in Ruby, Iditarod racers continued to pass through but the mood of people and event changed. The bustle and curiosity surrounding the front-runners had evaporated and by the time the midfield arrived, children were back in school, Ruby had reverted to its normal routine and the media had flown on to blunt their pencils at another checkpoint. Despondency hung over the dog teams resting on a quiet main street. These were the teams whose drivers had held higher expectations and one was Bill Cotter, lying in nineteenth place, with no more tricks up his mittens. 'I've put ten thousand bucks into this race and I'll be lucky to win five thousand in Nome,' he lamented. 'And it'll cost me another thousand to fly this outfit back from Nome.' He talked of quitting.

I prepared my own team for the resumption of our journey. We were all packed and ready. My dogs looked fresh and healthy compared with their racing colleagues, but in this respect my opinion was always biased. No one ever came up to me and made loud covetous noises about my companions, but they still made me brim with pride.

A thaw followed by a sudden freeze produces a hazardous running surface, and over twenty-four hours the Yukon basin experienced a 70° shift in temperature, from 45° F to –26° F. Ice crystals became sharp and abrasive, and quickly caused severe laceration to paw pads unless bootees were fitted. Bootees were small pouches of durable bunting, usually Polarfleece, worn like socks and held on with a wraparound of velcro. They had to be fitted tightly enough to stay on without restricting blood circulation.

Putting bootees on a whole team was no musher's idea of fun. Fingers got cold and had to be warmed after every one or two dogs. In cold weather it took me twenty minutes to bootee eight dogs. If the dogs rested for more than fifteen minutes, I had to loosen all thirty-two bootees. If the dogs ran through water, all bootees had to be changed. Polarfleece could be expected to last thirty or forty miles but footwear had to be checked regularly because a hole let in ice and rendered a bootee potentially *more* damaging to a dog's foot. They were a lot of work, and unpopular.

Silver hated wearing bootees. She always held up her first booteed foot as if I had just injured it. When I booteed the second, she disregarded the first and held up this newly damaged limb. With four bootees on she lay down, totally disabled. She had no fear of other dogs, glare ice, deep snow or wind, but she drew the line at footwear. And yet at the command to go she always leapt up and never gave them a second thought.

We made a handsome team – thirty-two feet in socks of red, blue or mock-tartan (and two more in bunny boots) – as we pulled out of Ruby at midday, gatecrashing Iditarod rankings in about thirtieth position. The trail was clearly marked by flags at one hundred yard intervals and these would continue all the way to Nome. It was marked by lost or discarded bootees even more regularly. I leaned over and snatched them up on the move, keeping only the best, for it appeared mushers had been reducing their loads and discarding unused bootees by the dozen. The novelty soon wore off even though – at seventy cents apiece – here were some of the richer pickings of the rush.

For fifteen miles we followed Ruby Slough and were sunk in a trough in spruce forest. Alf shied when we came to a parked snow machine and a man raising a beaver through a hole in the ice, and shied again when a whiskey jack (a species of jay also called, for its sins, 'camp robber') swooped low over us out of spite or boredom. When the trail turned off the slough we climbed a bank and ran through forest. It felt exhilarating to be on a trail wending through trees again but after a mile we emerged on to the expansive Yukon. A huddle of cabins soon appeared far off on our right. Whiskey Creek.

Alaskan 'water of life' was once produced here, uniquely and impatiently. The Bush distillers of Whiskey Creek wanted to speed up the maturation process and to this end they constructed a large water wheel. Full casks of spirit were strapped to the wheel and made to revolve constantly in the hope that it would do the trick. It didn't. This must have taken place before 1925, because by that year the creek's name was established; 'Whiskey Creek to Galena' was the Serum Run leg driven by Ed Nollner. In two days I hoped to meet him, because he still lived in Galena.

'HAW. Good girl.' When we were well clear of the trail we stopped for a rest. A fourteen-dog team approached from behind, an Austrian musher, it transpired, running the Great Race for the first time. The minimum credential required for a rookie musher to take part in the Iditarod was proof of having completed the course of any two-hundred-mile race. This rookie team plodded and looked exhausted. The lead dog tried to turn off the trail and follow my tracks. Horst Maas stamped on his brake and shouted 'GEE.' He repeated it again and again. The dog stood still and stared at me with a statue's pretence of vision. Then it slowly turned and moved off.

Horst looked along my line of dogs and stopped fifty yards later.

'All of them?' he called. 'I also must do?' He raised a boot, tapped it and pointed at my team.

'I'm not sure. I think this snow is bad for their feet.'

Only a few of his dogs wore bootees. He wrestled his shoulders inside his parka. 'It's very cold.' His voice came low and listless. I called 'Are you all right?' but he didn't hear me for he had already turned, and with much shouting the gloomy procession drew away. I stood lost in thought for a while. That lead dog's eyes . . . The Iditarod shed some of its glory in this brief encounter.

I spent the night camped in Jimmy Malamute's cabin. It earned one star through having a roof. Jimmy Malamute, whoever he was, had not maintained it for a long time. A quarter of one wall was missing and drifts had recreated the Alaskan landscape inside. If my sled had been able to negotiate the Yukon's steep bank I could have driven the team through the wall, across the floor and out the door. One advantage of this was that my snowshoes could stay on the whole time, and the surrounding snow was so deep and soft that it was impossible to do anything without them. I wore the Big Feet to relay my supplies up from the river, to picket the dogs, to gather wood and to cross the cabin to add salt to my porridge.

I found another advantage to wall-less cabins; if the views are good, they are unimpeded. The setting sun sent fingers of spruce shadow reaching across the Yukon and faintly pinked its surface. Willows on the far bank turned to rust and glowed. Across this scene, moving from right to left, a dog team travelled close to the middle of the river. It was no more than a silhouette of seven small dots in line and a large one misshapen at the rear. It moved steadily and silently, undulating over the bumps in the trail with mesmerising fluency. It looked so delicate when set in this vast billowing land, and yet in no time it had glided past and slipped out of sight.

When a second team passed I went for my camera. I could feel that the temperature was unusually cold but my camera showed me just how cold it was. Bush lore offered a cornucopia of crude devices for gauging temperature. Some worked on principles as extreme as a miner's dead canary. Others were more humane and discerning and one of the most famous was McQueston's thermometer. It was common knowledge among bushmen of the time that mercury solidified at –40° (Fahrenheit *and* Centigrade, for at this point the two scales intersect) and that pure alcohol, such as Davis Painkiller, froze at –70° F. Certain other commodities had freezing points in between. McQueston's thermometer consisted of four small bottles and a note of recommendations placed on a shelf outside his trading post. The bottles contained mercury, whisky, kerosene and Davis Painkiller. Travellers shook the bottles in sequence. If the mercury was frozen, the note recommended not being caught out on the trail at night; if the whisky, it was unwise to leave camp; if the kerosene, a person should not leave his cabin; and if Davis Painkiller turned to ice, it was dangerous to step away from the fire.

My thermometer was my camera. For it to function at all I had to use an external battery pack which I wore close to my body along with the daily ration of snacks. A cord from the battery pack had to be retrieved from my many layers and screwed into the camera each time it was used. If a film splintered and broke when I tried to wind it on to the next exposure, the temperature was −30° F or lower. This was the bottom end of my scale. That evening my film splintered and broke. I had to warm the camera by the fire and then remove the damaged film in the darkness of a sleeping bag.

It was even colder the next morning when I awoke. My sleeping bag enveloped me except where a small hole was allowed for breathing, and overnight this became a crust of ice. The moments contemplating getting up were always agonising, preparing to release the draw string and allowing in that shriek of cold. My bunny boots would have an ice lining from the previous day's perspiration, but there was a trick to eradicate this problem. I emptied a thermos of hot water into one boot, swilled it around, emptied it into the other, drained them both, leapt into them, donned parka, gloves and over-trousers, and then launched into a frenzy of physical jerks. Leaping up and down on the spot, swinging my arms in arcs and slapping myself on the back – this had to be done vigorously for several minutes. It was effective but painful. There is no way around this. Mushers come either battered or frozen.

In extreme cold everything became complex, stubborn or stuck. Simple tasks became protracted events and the least of them suddenly demanded the most testing degrees of dexterity. Every aspect of a routine now contrived to make you remove your gloves and when you finally succumbed, your fingers immediately chilled and your gloves froze to grotesque shapes. My solid-fuel hand-warmer reliably produced heat an hour after I needed it, my Coleman stove refused to work at all. It made me envy the dogs.

Snow would have settled on them during the night and by morning they would be hard to spot. One by one they would look up and shake their heads on hearing the commotion of my violent slapping. They would continue dozing and yet keep a periodic check on my progress, watching me blow into cupped hands as the fifth match expired before lighting the tinder and watching me generally fetch, saw, melt, stir, stoke, serve, tidy and pack. When they smelt their morning soup and snack coming, they would spring to life, rock back into the posture of an up-ended sphinx and luxuriate in a stretch. In twenty seconds they would devour what had taken me an hour and a half to prepare, and two minutes later they would be dozing again.

On cold mornings such as this one, when we were about to set off for Galena, my dogs depreciated. Anyone could have had them for a song, with harnesses thrown in.

# SOUTH AMERICA

## REDMOND O'HANLON

# IN TROUBLE AGAIN
## A Journey between the Orinoco and the Amazon

**E**ARLY IN THE afternoon we paddled into Toucan hill bend and made camp. Unlike the grand canyon of the great Neblina massif, it looked the kind of hillock that any fool could climb on all fours – and as we now had enough plantains and peach-palm nuts to feed a forestful of coati-mundis I decided that we would stay where we were for a day or two. Pablo took the gun and the curiara and set off downstream; Yavateiba took his bow and arrows and quiver and disappeared into the forest.

My right hand was now so swollen that I could not use it, and Juan slung my hammock for me. No sooner had I sat on its edge, rubbing more Anthisan into my puffy knuckles, than the trumpeter, released from his cage, rushed up to me and stood still at my feet, peep-peeping to have his head scratched. Flattered, I stroked him with my one serviceable index finger; the black feathers on top of his skull were short and nobbly to the touch. He stopped peeping, lifted one leg, and went into a trance. From the edge of his eyes nearest the beak the nicitating membranes, the third lids, moved slowly across his eyeballs until both lenses were entirely filmed over.

It was odd to think that almost nothing was known about the courtship and social behaviour in the wild of even this widely domesticated bird, kept as a snake-killer and alarm-caller. I stopped stroking and he withdrew his membranes, shook himself, fluffed out his wispy back-feathers and began a desultory scratching and pecking among the fallen leaves. However, now that he had made friends with me I kept half an eye on his movements, mindful of Spruce's experience:

> When at Panuré, on the river Uaupés, we had a tame agamí [trumpeter] which so attached itself to me that it would follow me about like a dog, and never failed to kill any snake that came in our way. One day I was alone with the agamí in a caatinga about four miles from the village, where I lingered about a good while in a spot comparatively clear of underwood, but abounding in certain minute plants (Burmanniaceae) which I was much interested to gather. Whilst I hunted for plants the agamí hunted for snakes, and had already caught three or four, which it brought and laid before me as it caught them. I suppose I had not noticed and praised its prowess as I usually did, for at length – apparently determined to attract my attention – it laid a newly-caught snake on my naked feet, when I was standing erect, absorbed in the examination of a little Burmannia with my lens. The snake was scarcely injured, and immediately twined up my leg. To snatch it off and jerk it away into the bush was the work of a moment; but ever afterwards I took care to leave the agamí at home when I started for the forest.

Chimo and the boy made a fire and boiled up the peach-palm fruit, and as night fell Pablo returned bearing a large cayman. Almost simultaneously Yavateiba stepped into the clearing. He carried his bow and arrows in one hand and a brace of trumpeters in the other. He bent down in front of his pet bird, made peeping noises, and, holding up the heads of his victims, pecked their beaks in the trumpeter's face. It redrew the membranes across its eyeballs.

The dead, glossy trumpeters seemed unmarked until I noticed that they were both bleeding from their anal vents. Yavateiba had shot them from behind with his thinnest arrow-tip – and it was just possible that he had deliberately hit them up the gut in order not to spoil the already small amount of meat on their bodies. To command such accuracy, I thought, must be one of the pleasures of being a Yanomami male: when he comes across a giant turtle basking in a lake, said Culimacaré, the Yanomami hunter stands on the bank and shoots an arrow into the air at just that angle which will bring it down to pierce the one weak spot in a turtle's shell, which lies, like the central suture on a baby's head, right in the centre of the carapace.

Pablo opened his cayman with the axe and laid it out along our plank seat in the dugout for disembowelling. Yavateiba and I went down to watch; when Pablo pulled out the coils of the large intestine and made as if to tumble them into the river Yavateiba jumped into the canoe and pushed him aside. He eased out the whole alimentary canal and climbed back up the bank with it slopped in his arms. Intrigued, I followed. By the fire he grasped one end of the fishy tube in his right hand and slowly pulled the whole length through the tight sphincter made by his fingers, squeezing out the grey sludge of half-made cayman shit. The boy disappeared briefly into the forest and came back with a few large leaves. Yavateiba then wrapped up the bundle of guts, secured it with a piece of vine, arranged one leaf at the side into a spout, and pushed the whole gently into the ashes at the edge of the fire.

We sat down to wait and in about five minutes Yavateiba decided it was ready; he pulled out the leaf vessel and held the spout in front of me; honoured, I opened my mouth and he tipped in half a cupful of liquid. It was warm, thick, slimy, like a mixture of cod-liver oil and the re-cycled juice from old sardine tins. Yavateiba ministered likewise to Maquichemi, Jarivanau and the boy, finished the rest himself and threw the leaves and guts into the undergrowth.

Abducting Chimo's torch, Juan looked through his interminable notes on the carbon content of the tierra firme, caatinga and riparial forests of the Rio Negro, Casiquiare, Pasimoni, Baria and Emoni rivers. Galvis plucked, gutted and jointed the trumpeters and added them to the peach-palm stew. Valentine and Culimacaré built a smoking rack for Pablo's cayman and Yavateiba purloined the cayman's head. He pushed it, too, into the fire, and when it was cooked he and Maquichemi extracted the small, backwardly curved, yellowish teeth and stowed them in one of their baskets. They then hacked open the skull with a machete and ate the brains.

It was the beginning of a feast; later that night we gorged ourselves on stringy peach-palm fruit and even stringier little bits of trumpeter meat; we ate Jarivanau's baked plantains and we chewed pieces of cayman which he skewered on sticks and placed upright in a ring round the fire. Chimo and Valentine swapped stories. There was a man in Brazil, said Valentine, who had set the stone from the head of an electric eel into his hand: whenever he punched someone, he electrocuted them. That was nothing, said Chimo, there was a hill somewhere near here that was made entirely of gold. His father had told him about it before he died. You'd know when you were close: if you shot a curassow and when you went to pick it up you found that its legs were gold, you were close all right – that bird had spent its life treading in gold dust.

'Reymono,' said Culimacaré from his hammock, 'where are aeroplanes made?'

'All over the world. They even make them in Brazil.'

'Then that is where I would like to go,' he said quietly. 'I would like to go where aeroplanes are made and learn to be a pilot. I would like to fly over the trees.'

Jarivanau, bored of all the talk which he could not understand, gave me a conspiratorial smile, walked casually over to my bergen, undid the ties and took out Schauensee as if he owned it. He carried the book back to Yavateiba, Maquichemi and the boy, and huddled them up closer to the fire. Very slowly, he turned over the plates.

I went and sat beside him. Yavateiba grew increasingly excited, talking very fast in his stressed language. A great naming of birds in Yanomami took place; they seemed to know almost every bird in Amazonas; and when Jarivanau reached Kathleen Phelps's painting of the cotingas it was obvious that Yavateiba was as entranced by it as I was: he leant forward to look more closely and called softly to himself: *hudu! hudu!* for the blue-crowned motmot; a sequence of differently pitched bellows for the Amazonian umbrellabird, the red-ruffled fruitcrow and the capuchinbird; a high *krioow* for the cock-of-the-rock and a quack whose supposed author escaped me.

Unwittingly, I brought the party to an end by taking the book and flicking through the black and white drawings from the back to the front. Yavateiba shook his head at pictures of the gulls and terns of Venezuela's Caribbean coast and by the time we came to the figure of Leach's storm-petrel and the dusky-backed shear-water his faith in the book of the *nabë*, the foreigner, the non-Yanomami, the non-human being, had obviously evaporated. He did not believe it. Yavateiba did not believe in the sea.

As Juan and I lay in our hammocks preparing to go to sleep – in my case I had reached the stage of plumping up my pillow, or restuffing my torn shirt in a half-rotted pair of blue Y-fronts of which I had grown inordinately fond – a shadow launched itself from a small tree behind our heads and landed with an appreciable thud on the leaf litter between us. Juan, who still had Chimo's torch, leant over the side of his hammock and shone it at the ground.

In the circle of weak light there was something flattish, motionless, dinner-plate-size, furry, brown.

'Quick!' yelled Juan suddenly. 'It's a tarantula!'

But it was not the much smaller animal which tarantula signifies in English. I realised, with a rush of adrenalin, that I was looking at the largest spider in the world, the bird-eating spider, whose habits Maria Sibilla Merian, an artist working in Dutch Guiana, was the first to describe and paint in her book *Metamorphosis Insectorum Surinamensium* (1705). Her spider has an unlikely looking hummingbird by the throat and is dragging it from its pill-box nest. Everyone ridiculed her account until at Cametá, on the Tocantins river in Brazil, Bates chanced to verify a fact relating to the habits of a large hairy spider of the genus Mygale, in a manner worth recording. The species was M. avicularia, or one very closely allied to it; the individual was nearly two inches in length of body, but the legs expanded seven inches, and the entire body and legs were covered with coarse grey and reddish hairs. I was attracted by a movement of the monster on a tree-trunk; it was close beneath a deep crevice in the tree, across which was stretched a dense white web. The lower part of the web was broken, and two small birds, finches, were entangled in the pieces; they were about the size of the English siskin, and I judged the two to be male and female. One of them was quite dead, the other lay under the body of the spider not quite dead, and was smeared with the filthy liquor or saliva exuded by the monster. I drove away the spider and took the birds, but the second one soon died. The fact of species of Mygale sallying forth at night, mounting trees, and sucking the eggs and young of humming-birds, has been recorded long ago by Madam Merian and Palisot de Beauvois; but, in the absence of any confirmation, it has come to be discredited . . . Some Mygales are of immense size. One day I saw the children belonging to an Indian family, who collected for me, with one of these monsters secured by a cord round its waist, by which they were leading it about the house as they would a dog.

Bates's monster was probably a female, the web an old cocoon and the crevice just a lair to which the finches had been dragged, because bird-eating spiders do not generally build webs but run their prey down in quick dashes along branches or on the ground at night. The Yanomami are said to eat their legs roasted, but obviously not after a banquet of peach-palm fruit and cayman pieces – Jarivanau crept up behind it, very warily, and hit it once with a long pole.

'They can jump three metres from standing,' said Juan. 'They inject you with a powerful enzyme which digests the flesh – and be careful in the morning, Redmon, because all the hairs on their bodies are poisonous.'

The camp settled down again. A marbled wood-quail began to crow like a rooster. A black-and-white owl called his explosive, deep, dismissive, single *boo* every ten to twenty seconds from somewhere nearby. I fell asleep and dreamed, not of becoming a milkshake for spiders, as I expected, but of Kellaways. I was back, eight years old, on another family expedition to the Avon. We carried the two-seater canvas canoe through the archway, across the fields, and lowered it into the river. As usual, my father and I paddled upstream. At the fifteenth bend the unreachable railway bridge came into view through the gap in the stand of bullrushes, unimaginably far away from the landing-stage and the picnic basket behind us. Yet this time we did not turn back; my father kept paddling and, three bends later, there was the bridge ahead of us. But as we approached the pitted stone pillars and the rusty iron girders they slowly metamorphosed into a line of poles supported by sapling X-frames and handrails of liana. We passed beneath it; and suddenly I was suffused with an intense happiness.

In the morning, as soon as it was light enough to see properly, Pablo took the gun and paddled downstream in the curiara, and I borrowed Juan's scissors, wrapped my left hand in a leaf, straightened out the mangled body of the spider and cut away its long brown fangs, tough as crab-shell. I dropped them into one of Juan's plastic bags and stowed it in my bergen.

Trumpeter feathers from Galvis's plucking pile were drifting gently about over the rotting leaves, propelled by the tiny breezes that got up as a few oblique lines of sunlight filtered down to the jungle floor and spotted it with warmth. I picked up three breast feathers and laid them in my notebook. Delicate, fan-shaped, they appeared to be a uniform grey when lying flat on the page, but when held at an angle to one of the neighbouring lines of light, each feather shone at its top with a crescent of purple whose inside edge was radiant with minute bands of green and orange and gold.

There was a loud bang and ten minutes later an excited Pablo pulled into the bank.

'Now we have meat for days and days,' he shouted.

'Take it easy,' said Chimo, 'you'll upset the boat.'

A huge, wet capybara, the world's largest rodent, lay in the bow of the curiara. Chimo and Culimacaré helped Pablo lift it ashore. About four feet long, a male, its deep, massive body was covered in grey-brown, bristly hairs, and its short legs ended in four partially webbed toes on the front feet and three on the back. Its nostrils and eyes and little rounded ears were set high on its broad, squarish head, further adaptations for its semi-aquatic life. Chimo and Pablo butchered it and gave me the two cheek-teeth from its upper jaw. Backwardly curved to unequal degrees so that one was almost semicircular, they were yellowish white with a shallow groove down the centre of their front surfaces, worn to a sharp, angled cutting edge and, as measured by Juan's ruler, they were three and a half inches long.

Valentine stoked up the wood under the smoking-rack and moved the remains of the cayman tail to one side. Jarivanau skewered slabs of muscle and fat on sticks and sat down to monitor his roasting system, a fence of meat around the fire. Yavateiba commandeered the offal, but instead of squeezing out the intestines he lodged all the guts at the edge of the river on the upstream side of a half-submerged log, fetched one of Chimo's lines, baited the hook with bits of capybara skin and began to pull in furiously thrashing piranha, their backs dark blue, the small scales on their flanks sparks of silver.

After a slow, remarkably quiet breakfast of capybara chunks, which tasted like sirloin-on-the-bone, Pablo, Chimo and Valentine wandered off into the forest to find exactly the right kind of buttresses from which to carve four more paddles – so that we could all help propel the dugouts down the Siapa if the one tankful of petrol should prove insufficient to force us clear of the blackfly; Maquichemi took her son to play in Galvis's part of the canoe, where he had stored all the empty plastic containers that had once held oats and all the sounding tins that had once been full to the brim with crude brown sugar; Galvis himself settled down on his medicine chest to read about unarmed resistance with Mahatma Gandhi; and Yavateiba, Jarivanau, the boy, Juan and I set off to climb Toucan hill.

PAUL THEROUX

# THE OLD PATAGONIAN EXPRESSS
## By Train through the Americas

**T**HE SAN SALVADOR railway station was at the end of a torn-up section of road in a grim precinct of the city. My ticket was collected by a man in a porkpie hat and sports shirt, who wore an old-fashioned revolver on his hip. The station was no more than a series of cargo sheds, where very poor people were camped, waiting for the morning train to Cutuco: the elderly and the very young – it seemed to be the pattern of victims in Central American poverty. Alfredo had given me the name of a hotel and said he would meet me there an hour before kickoff, which was nine o'clock. The games were played late, he said, because by then it wasn't so hot. But it was now after dark, and the humid heat still choked me. I began to wish that I had not left Santa Ana. San Salvador, prone to earthquakes, was not a pretty place; it sprawled, it was noisy, its buildings were charmless, and in the glare of headlights were buoyant particles of dust. Why would anyone come here? 'Don't knock it,' an American in San Salvador told me. 'You haven't seen Nicaragua yet!'

Alfredo was late. He blamed the traffic: 'There will be a million people at the stadium.' He had brought along some friends, two boys who, he boasted, were studying English.

'How are you doing?' I asked them in English.

'Please?' said one. The other laughed. The first one said in Spanish, 'We are only on the second lesson.'

Because of the traffic, and the risk of car thieves at the stadium, Alfredo parked a half mile away, at a friend's house. This

144

house was worth some study; it was a number of cubicles nailed to trees, with the leafy branches depending into the rooms. Cloth was hung from sticks to provide walls, and a strong fence surrounded it. I asked the friend how long he had lived there. He said his family had lived in the house for many years. I did not ask what happened when it rained.

But poverty in a poor country had subtle gradations. We walked down a long hill, toward the stadium, and crossing a bridge I looked into a gorge, expecting to see a river, and saw lean-tos and cooking fires and lanterns. Who lives there? I asked Alfredo.

'Poor people,' he said.

Others were walking to the stadium, too. We joined a large procession of quick-marching fans, and as we drew closer to the stadium they began yelling and shoving in anticipation. The procession swarmed over the foothills below the stadium, crashing through people's gardens and thumping the fenders of stalled cars. Here the dust was deep, and the trampling feet of the fans made it rise until it became a brown fog, like a sepia print of a mob scene, with the cones of headlights bobbing in it. The mob was running now, and Alfredo and his friends were obscured by the dust cloud. Every ten feet, boys rushed forward and shook tickets at me, screaming, 'Suns! Suns! Suns!'

These were the touts. They bought the cheapest tickets and sold them at a profit to people who had neither the time nor the courage to stand in a long rowdy line at a ticket window. The seat designations were those usual at a bullfight: 'Suns' were the cheapest bleacher seats; 'Shades' were more expensive ones under the canopy.

I fought my way through the touts and, having lost Alfredo, made my way uphill to the kettle-shaped stadium. It was an unearthly sight; the crowd of people emerging from darkness into luminous brown fog, the yells, the dust rising, the mountainside smouldering under a sky which, because of the dust, was starless. At that point I considered turning back; but the mob was propelling me forward toward the stadium, where the roar of the spectators inside made a sound like flames howling in a chimney.

145

The mob took up this cry and surged past me, stirring up the dust. There were women frying bananas and meat pies over fires on the walkway that ran around the outside perimeter of the stadium. The smoke from these fires and the dust made each searchlight seem to burn with a smoky flame. The touts reappeared nearer the stadium. They were hysterical now. The game was about to start; they had not sold their tickets. They grabbed my arms, they pushed tickets in my face, they shouted.

One look at the lines of people near the ticket windows told me that I would have no chance at all of buying a ticket legally. I was pondering this question when, through the smoke and dust, Alfredo appeared.

'Take your watch off,' he said. 'And your ring. Put them in your pocket. Be very careful. Most of these people are thieves. They will rob you.'

I did as I was told. 'What about the tickets? Shall we buy some Suns from these boys?'

'No, I will buy Shades.'

'Are they expensive?'

'Of course, but this will be a great game. I could never see such a game in Santa Ana. Anyway, the Shades will be quieter.' Alfredo looked around. 'Hide over there by the wall. I will get the tickets.'

Alfredo vanished into the conga line at a ticket window. He appeared again at the middle of the line, jumped the queue, elbowed forward, and in a very short time had fought his way to the window. Even his friends marvelled at his speed. He came toward us smiling, waving the tickets in triumph.

We were frisked at the entrance; we passed through a tunnel and emerged at the end of the stadium. From the outside it had looked like a kettle; inside, its shape was more of a salver, a tureen filled with brown screeching faces. In the centre was a pristine rectangle of green grass.

It was, those 45,000 people, a model of Salvadorean society. Not only the half of the stadium where the Suns sat (and it was jammed: not an empty seat was visible); or the better-dressed and almost as crowded half of the Shades (at night, in the dry season,

146

there was no difference in the quality of the seats: we sat on concrete steps, but ours, being more expensive than the Suns, were less crowded); there was a section that Alfredo had not mentioned: the Balconies. Above us, in five tiers of a gallery that ran around our half of the stadium, were the Balcony people. Balcony people had season tickets. Balcony people had small rooms, closet-sized, about as large as the average Salvadorean's hut; I could see the wine bottles, the glasses, the plates of food. Balcony people had folding chairs and a good view of the field. There were not many Balcony people – two or three hundred – but at $2,000 for a season ticket in a country where the annual per capita income was $373, one could understand why. The Balcony people faced the screaming Suns and, beyond the stadium, a plateau. What I took to be lumpish multicoloured vegetation covering the plateau was, I realised, a heap of Salvadoreans standing on top or clinging to the sides. There were thousands of them in this mass, and it was a sight more terrifying than the Suns. They were lighted by the stadium glare; there was a just-perceptible crawling movement among the bodies; it was an anthill.

National anthems were played, amplified songs from scratched records, and then the game began. It was apparent from the outset who would win. Mexico was bigger, faster, and seemed to follow a definite strategy; El Salvador had two ball-hoggers, and the team was tiny and erratic. The crowd hissed the Mexicans and cheered El Salvador. One of the Salvadorean ball-hoggers went jinking down the field, shot and missed. The ball went to the Mexicans, who tormented the Salvadoreans by passing it from man to man, and then, fifteen minutes into the game, the Mexicans scored. The stadium was silent as the Mexican players kissed one another.

Some minutes later the ball was kicked into the Shades section. It was thrown back on to the field, and the game was resumed. Then it was kicked into the Suns section. The Suns fought for it. One man gained possession, but he was pounced upon and the ball shot up and ten Suns went tumbling after it. A Sun tried to run down the steps with it. He was caught and the ball wrestled from him. A fight began, and now there were scores of Suns punching their way to the ball. The Suns higher up in the section threw bottles and cans and wadded paper on the Suns who were fighting, and the shower of objects – meat pies, bananas, hankies – continued to fall. The Shades, the Balconies, the Anthill, watched this struggle.

And the players watched, too. The game had stopped. The Mexican players kicked the turf, the Salvadorean team shouted at the Suns.

*Please return the ball.* It was the announcer. He was hoarse. *If the ball is not returned, the game will not continue.*

This brought a greater shower of objects from the upper seats – cups, cushions, more bottles. The bottles broke with a splashing sound on the concrete seats. The Suns lower down began throwing things back at their persecutors, and it was impossible to say where the ball had gone.

The ball was not returned. The announcer repeated his threat.

The players sat down on the field and did limbering-up exercises until, ten minutes after the ball had disappeared from the field, a new ball was thrown in. The spectators cheered but, just as quickly, fell silent. Mexico had scored another goal.

Soon, a bad kick landed the ball into the Shades. This ball was fought for and not thrown back, and one could see the ball progressing through the section. The ball was seldom visible, but one could tell from the free-for-alls – now here, now there – where it was. The Balconies poured water on the Shades, but the ball was not surrendered. And now it was the Suns' turn to see the slightly better-off Salvadoreans in the Shades section behaving like swine. The announcer made his threat: the game would not resume until the ball was thrown back. The threat was ignored, and after a long time the ref walked on to the field with a new ball.

In all, five balls were lost this way. The fourth landed not far from where I sat, and I could see that real punches were being thrown, real blood spurting from Salvadorean noses, and the broken bottles and the struggle for the ball made it a contest all its own, more savage than the one on the field, played out with the kind of mindless ferocity you read about in books on gory medieval sports. The anouncer's warning was merely ritual threat; the police did not intervene – they stayed on the field and let the spectators settle their own scores. The players grew bored: they ran in place, they did pushups. When play resumed and Mexico gained possession of the ball, it deftly moved down the field and invariably made a goal. But this play, these goals – they were no more than interludes in a much bloodier sport which, toward midnight (and the game was still not over!), was varied by Suns throwing firecrackers at each other and on to the field.

The last time play was abandoned and fights broke out among the Suns – the ball bobbing from one ragged Sun to another – balloons were released from the upper seats. But they were not balloons. They were white, blimpy, and had a nipple on the end; first one, then dozens. This caused great laughter, and they were batted from section to section. They were of course contraceptives, and they caused Alfredo no end of embarrassment. 'That is very bad,' he said, gasping in shame. He had apologised for the interruptions; for the fights; the delayed play. Now this – dozens of airborne rubbers. The game was a shambles; it ended in confusion, fights, litter. But it shed light on the recreations of Salvadoreans. And as for the other thing – the inflated contraceptives – I later discovered that the Agency for International Development's largest Central American family-planning program is in El Salvador. I doubt whether the birthrate has been affected, but children's birthday parties in rural El Salvador must be a great deal of fun, what with the free balloons.

Mexico won the game, six to one. Alfredo said that El Salvador's goal was the best one of the game, a header from thirty yards. So he managed to rescue a shred of pride. But people had been leaving all through the second half, and the rest hardly seemed to notice or to care that the game had ended. Just before we left the stadium I looked up at the anthill. It was a hill once again; there were no people on it, and, depopulated, it seemed very small.

Outside, on the stadium slopes, the scene was like one of those lurid murals of hell you see in Latin American churches. The colour was infernal, yellow dust sifted and whirled among crater-like pits, small cars with demonic headlights moved slowly from hole to hole like mechanical devils. And where, on the murals, you would see the signs printed and dramatised, the gold lettering saying LUST, ANGER, AVARICE, DRUNKENNESS, GLUTTONY, THEFT, PRIDE, JEALOUSY, USURY, GAMBLING, here, after midnight, were groups of boys lewdly snatching at girls, and knots of people fighting, counting the money they had won, staggering and swigging from bottles, shrieking obscenities against Mexico, thumping the hoods of cars, or duelling with the branches they had yanked from trees and the radio aerials they had twisted from cars. They trampled the dust and howled. The car horns were like harsh moos of pain, and one car was being overturned by a gang of shirtless, sweating youths. Many people were running to get free of the mob, holding hankies over their faces. But there were tens of thousands of people here, and animals, too – maimed dogs snarling and cowering as in a classic vision of hell. And it was hot: dark grimy air that was hard to breathe and freighted with the stinks of sweat; it was so thick it muted the light. It tasted of stale fire and ashes. The mob did not disperse; it was too angry to go home, too insulted by defeat to ignore its hurt. It was loud, and it moved as if thwarted and pushed; it danced madly in what seemed a deep hole.

Alfredo knew a short cut to the road. He led the way through the parking lot and a ravaged grove of trees behind some huts. I saw people lying on the ground, but whether they were wounded or sleeping or dead I could not tell.

I asked him about the mob.

'What did I tell you?' he said. 'You are sorry you came, right?'

'No,' I said, and I meant it. Now I was satisfied. Travel is pointless without certain risks. I had spent the whole evening scrutinising what I saw, trying to memorise details, and I knew I would never go to another soccer game in Latin America.

TOM MILLER

# THE PANAMA HAT TRAIL
## A Journey from South America

T O REACH THE TOWN of Febres Cordero I took a bus to Guayaquil – at 1.6 million, the country's most populous city. The 150-mile ride started smoothly despite my apprehension. Bus rides through Latin America have always induced fear in me, brought on by years of reading one-paragraph bus-plunge stories used by newspapers in the States as fillers on the foreign-news page. The datelines change, but the headlines always include the words *bus plunge*, as in 12 DIE IN SRI LANKA BUS PLUNGE, or CHILEAN BUS PLUNGE KILLS 31. 'We can count on one every couple of days or so,' an editor at the *New York Times* once told me. 'They're always ready when we need them.' Never more than two sentences long, a standard bus-plunge piece will usually include the number feared dead, the identity of any group on board – a soccer team, church choir or school bus – and the distance of the plunge from the capital city. The words *ravine* and *gorge* pop up often. Most of the stories come from Third World countries, the victims comprising just a fraction of the faceless brown-skinned masses. 'A hundred Pakistanis going off a mountain in a bus make less of a story than three Englishmen drowning in the Thames,' noted foreign correspondent Mort Rosenblum in *Coups & Earthquakes*. Is there a news service that does nothing but supply daily papers with bus-plunge stories? Peru and India seem to generate the most coverage; perhaps the wire services have more stringers in the Andes and Himalayas than anywhere else.

If an Ecuadorian bus driver survives a plunge fatal to others, according to Moritz Thomsen in *Living Poor*, 'he immediately goes into hiding in some distant part of the country so that the bereaved can't even up the score. There are rumours of whole villages down in the far reaches of the Amazon basin populated almost entirely by bus drivers. This is probably apocryphal . . .'

If you anticipate a bus trip in Latin America, go through the following checklist prior to boarding:

- Look at the tyres. If three or more of the six tyres (most buses include two rear sets of two each) are totally bald, the probability of bus plunge increases. Visible threads on the tyres means a blowout is imminent.
- Does the bus have at least one windshield wiper? Good. If it's on the driver's side, so much the better. Try to avoid buses whose windshields are so crowded with decals, statues and pictures that the driver has only a postcard-sized hole through which to see the future. Shrines to saints, pious homilies, boastful bumper stickers and religious trinkets do not reflect the safety of a bus. Jesus Christ and Ché Guevara are often worshipped on the same decal. This should give neither high hopes nor nagging suspicion.
- The driver's sobriety isn't a factor. The presence of his wife or girlfriend is. If she's along, she will usually sit immediately behind him, next to him, or on his lap. He will want to impress her with his daring at the wheel, but he will also go to great lengths not to injure her. If he has no girlfriend or wife, the chances of gorge-dive increase.
- You can't check the bus for brakes. Once I asked a driver in Guatemala about the brakes on his bus. 'Look,' he said, 'the bus is stopped, isn't it? Then the brakes must work.'
- On intercity buses, seats are often assigned before boarding. Refuse the seat directly behind the driver or in the front right. If your ride takes place during the day, you'll be subjected to at least one heart-skip a minute as your bus casually passes a truck on an uphill blind curve or goes head-to-head with an

oncoming bus. At night, the constant glare of approaching headlights will shine in your eyes. At any hour, the driver's makeshift radio speaker will dangle closer to your ears than you'd like.

• Always have your passport ready. Random military inspections take place when you least expect them. I once delayed a bus full of cross-country travellers for ten minutes a couple of miles outside Esmeraldas, on the Pacific Coast south of Colombia, while frantically searching first for my bag atop the bus, then my passport within the bag.

In defence of Latin-American buses: they go everywhere. *Everywhere*. No road is so dusty, bumpy, unpopulated, narrow or obscure that a bus doesn't rumble down it at least once every twenty-four hours. The fare is very little – Cuenca to Guayaquil cost less than three dollars – and, barring plunges, they almost always reach their destination. If your window opens, you'll get a view of the countryside unmatched in painting or postcard. Your seatmate may be an ageing *campesina* on her way home or a youthful Indian on his first trip to the big city. Dialects of Spanish and Quichua unknown to linguists float past you. Chickens, piglets and children crowd the aisles or ride on top.

At Cuenca's *terminal terrestre*, the bus station, I had a choice of taking a regular bus or an *aerotaxi* to Guayaquil. The former travels slower, hence theoretically safer. The latter, a small twenty-four-seater, whizzes along far faster, has less leg room, and is more plunge-prone. I resisted the odds and took an *aerotaxi*.

The trip, five and a half hours long, begins at eighty-four hundred feet above sea level, climbs somewhat higher, and descends to a sea level straightaway for the final ninety minutes or so. The advantage of the drive toward Guayaquil is that the precipitous ravine usually falls off on the left side of the two-lane road; the disadvantage is that you're headed downhill most of the way. Guard railings, few and far between, relieved a bit of my fear, except when the downhill section was bent outward or was simply broken off. For the better part of the first hour we followed a cattle truck, which moved only slightly faster than its cargo could have managed on its own.

The cattle turned off at Azogues, and we pushed on deep into the province of Cañar. The temperature dropped. I looked out the left side on to the clouds surrounding peaks nearby and distant. The thin air above the clouds in the Andes gave the sunlight colours unknown below. Only occasionally did our driver attempt a suicide squeeze – overtaking someone around a blind curve – and we settled into a quiet passage. Crude signs advertised local cheeses. Small piles of *toquilla* straw lay on the ground near doorless houses where women sat in the entrances weaving Panama hats. Julio, the driver, knew all the potholes and bumps on that road and managed to hit every one. Pepe, his helper – the driver's assistant is almost always a younger brother, son or nephew – fidgeted with the radio until he found a distant station whose static muffled a brass band. We passed Cañari Indians heading home; in front the father, directly behind him his wife, behind her a passel of kids, and bringing up the rear a burro and a goat. Each party in the procession was connected to the one behind by a rope tied around the midsection. A dog yipped alongside.

We descended into the thick of the clouds and Julio downshifted. The white line down the centre of the curving two-lane road was his only guide; even the hood ornament had disappeared into the clouds. After five minutes he slowed further and then stopped. Pepe walked through the *aerotaxi* collecting money. I nudged Horacio next to me. 'What's this for?'

'We're at the shrine,' he replied. 'Each driver stops at this shrine along the way and leaves some money. It's their way of asking God's blessings for a safe journey.' Often the saints are next to a police checkpoint so that the driver can make two payoffs at once. Offering insurance money to some saint required a gargantuan leap of faith, but if it would assure us a trip free of bus plunge, I wanted in. I coughed up a few sucres.

Pepe trotted across the road to leave our money at the shrine when suddenly a half-dozen Indian faces appeared out of the clouds pressing against the windows. '¡Choclos! ¡Choclos! ¡Diez *cada uno!'* They were selling sweet corn cooked with onion, cheese and egg for slightly more than ten cents each. Two barefoot Indian women in felt hats and thick mud-stained ponchos slipped on to the bus and walked up and down the aisle. *'¡Choclos! ¡Choclos! ¡Nueve cada uno!'* The price had gone down some. Another vendor with a glazed look in her eyes and a baby in her arms rapped desperately on a window trying to get a passenger to open it. Her shrill voice seemed as distant as her eyes. Pepe returned, and the Indians withdrew into the Andean mist.

Bus drivers' assistants throughout Latin America display keen skills at hopping on and off moving buses, keeping track of which passenger is due how much change for his fare, pumping gas, climbing through a window to the roof to retrieve some freight before the bus stops, and changing blowouts. Pepe performed all these feats in the course of the run to Guayaquil, and excelled at hopping on the bus when it was already in second gear. Trotting apace of the bus, he first took a short skip on the ground to get the spring in his feet, then a short jump at a forty-five-degree angle calculated to land him on the first step while he grasped a metal bar next to the doorway. His motion appeared so fluid and effortless, he seemed to be simply stepping on to a bus in repose.

The right rear tyre blew out on the southern edge of the town of Cañar. Julio pulled into an abandoned service station and Pepe had us back on the road within ten minutes. In more restful moments he sat on a makeshift seat between Julio and the door. The only job forbidden him was highway driving, and even then he was allowed to manoeuvre the bus around the terminals.

The ride down the western face of the Andes settled into a relatively peaceful journey once the tyre was changed and the saint paid off. We went through long stretches where the only hint of life was an occasional *choza*, a straw thatched hut, set back from the road. Valleys with streams and rivers flowing toward the Pacific held small towns. Our descent to sea level was practically complete and we entered a different climate, province, and culture. Bribing the saint had worked; we had passed the bus-plunge zone safely.

155

The air hung heavier, more humid, and warmer. Roadside vegetation grew more lush. Thick grass grew right up to roadside. Towns suddenly burst upon the highway – healthy, lively towns, active, jumping, noisy, uncaring. A church was just another building near the plaza, nothing more. Men and boys wore shorts, thongs and torn T-shirts. Women and girls wore slacks or short, loose cotton dresses. Card tables were surrounded by men who looked like they'd sat there months on end encircled by a floating crowd of onlookers. Shot glasses of *puro* were constantly drained and refilled. Every structure was made of bamboo – split, dry and aged. There was loud laughter, backslapping, gold-toothed grins, ass-pinching, life with few worries and less money. We had encountered our first *costeños* – people who live in the coastal region. Julio raced to Guayaquil on a road studded with potholes bigger than our *aerotaxi*. The tropics had begun.

## JOE SIMPSON

# TOUCHING THE VOID

WE HAD LEFT the snow hole at seven thirty, and two and a half hours later I could see that our progress was painfully slow. Since leaving the summit the previous afternoon we had descended no more than 1,000 feet instead of getting all the way down to the glacier in the six hours which we had reckoned. I began to feel impatient. I was tired of this grinding need to concentrate all the time. The mountain had lost its excitement, its novelty, and I wanted to get off it as soon as possible. The air was bitingly cold and the sky cloudless; the sun burnt down in a dazzling glare on the endless snow and ice. As long as we were back on the glacier before the afternoon storms I didn't care a damn what the weather chose to do.

At last the twisting mayhem of the upper ridge eased, and I could walk upright across the broad level ridge which undulated away in whale-backed humps towards the drop at its northern end. Simon caught up with me as I rested on my sack. We didn't speak. The morning had already taken its toll, and there was nothing left to say. Looking up at our footsteps weaving an unsteady path down towards us, I vowed silently to be more careful about checking descent routes in future.

I shouldered my sack and set off again, with no qualms about being in front now. I had wanted Simon to lead on the last stretch but had been unable to voice my apprehension and feared his response to it more than I feared another sickening fall. Deep snow had built up on the wide, level saddle, and, instead of anxiety

157

swamping my every move I was back to the frustration of wallowing through powder snow.

I had run out the rope, and Simon was getting up to follow when I stepped into the first crevasse.

In a rushing drop, I suddenly found myself standing upright but with my eyes level with the snow. The shallow fissure was filled with powder, so that however hard I thrashed about I seemed to make no upward movement at all. Eventually I managed to haul myself back on to level ground. From a safe distance Simon had watched my struggles with a grin on his face. I moved farther along the ridge and sank down again neck-deep in the snow. I yelled and cursed as I clawed my way back on to the ridge and, by the time I had traversed half-way across the plateau above it, I had fallen into another four small crevasses. However hard I tried, I could not see any tell-tale marks indicating their presence. Simon was following a full rope's-length behind. Frustration and the mounting exhaustion maddened me to a fury which I knew would be vented on Simon if he came close enough.

Then, crouching beside the hole I had just made, trying to regain my breath, I glanced back and was shocked to see clear through the ridge into the yawning abyss below. Blue-white light gleamed up through the hole from the expanse of the West Face, which I could see looming beneath it. Suddenly it clicked in my brain why I had fallen through so many times. It was all one crevasse, one long fracture line cutting right through the enormous humping cornices that made up the plateau. I moved quickly away to the side and shouted a warning to Simon. The rolling ridge had been so wide and flat it had never occurred to me that we might actually be standing on an overhanging cornice, one as large as the summit cornice, but stretching for several hundred feet. If it had collapsed we would have gone with it.

I kept well back from the edge after that, leaving a healthy margin of fifty feet. Simon had fallen with the smaller cornice collapse when he was forty feet back from the edge. There was no point in taking chances now that the flutings on the east side had eased into a uniformly smooth slope. My legs felt leaden trudging through the deep snow towards the end of the plateau. As I crested the last rise in the ridge and glanced back, I saw Simon hauling himself along in the same head-down, dog-tired manner as myself, a full rope's-length from me, 150 feet away, and I knew he would be out of sight once I began descending the long easy-angled slope ahead.

I had hoped to see the slope run down to the col but was disappointed to find it rising slightly to a minor summit of cornices before dropping steeply down again. Even so, I could see enough of the South Ridge of Yerupaja to know that the col would certainly lie immediately below that next drop, and then we would be at the lowest point on the ridge connecting Yerupaja and Siula Grande. Another half-hour would put us on that col, and it would be easy going from there to the glacier. I perked up.

Starting down, I felt at once the change in angle. It was so much easier than the plod along the saddle, and I would have romped happily down the gentle slope but for the rope tugging insistently at my waist. I had forgotten that Simon would still be wearily following my tracks on the saddle.

I had expected to be able to take a direct line to the small rise without encountering any obstacles, and was surprised to find that the slope ended abruptly in an ice cliff. It cut right across my path at right angles, bisecting the ridge. I approached the edge cautiously, and peered over a twenty-five-foot drop. The slope at its base swept down to the right in a smooth, steeply angled face. Beyond that lay the last rise on the ridge, about 200 feet away. The height of the cliff increased rapidly as it cut away from the ridge. I stood roughly mid-point on this wedge of ice running across the ridge, with its narrow edge abutting the ridge line. I traversed carefully away from the ridge, occasionally looking over the cliff to see if there was any weakness in the wall, which stood thirty-five feet high at its end. I had already discounted the possibility of abseiling past the cliff, for the snow at the top of the cliff was too loose to take an ice stake.

There were two options open to me. Either I could stay on the ridge top or I could continue away from it and hope to by-pass the steep section by a wide descending traverse. From where I stood at the end of the cliff I could see that this would be very tiring and risky. We would have to detour in a wide arc down, across, and then back up again, to by-pass the cliff. The initial slope down looked very steep and very unstable. I had had enough of slip-sliding around this ridge, and the empty sweep thousands of feet into the eastern glacier bay below the slope nudged me into decision. If either of us fell we would be on open slopes. We wouldn't stop. At least on the ridge we had been able to kid ourselves that we could, with luck, jump either side of the apex in the event of a fall.

I retraced my steps, intending to climb down the cliff at the easiest point. I knew this would be impossible near the crest of the ridge since there it was a near-vertical wall of powder snow. I needed to find a weakness in the cliff, a ramp line or a crevasse running down the cliff to give me some purchase on the ice, which appeared solid to within a few yards of the edge of the ridge. At last I saw what I was looking for – a very slight break in the angle of the ice wall. This part of the cliff was still steep, nearly vertical, but not quite. It was about twenty feet high at the break and I felt sure that at this point a few quick moves of reverse climbing would see me past the problem.

Crouching down on my knees, I turned my back to the cliff edge and managed to get my axes to bite in deeply. Slowly, I lowered my legs over the cliff until the edge was against my stomach and I could kick my crampons into the ice wall below me. I felt them bite and hold. Removing one axe, I hammered it in again very close to the edge. It held fast and solid. I removed my ice hammer and lowered my chest and shoulders over the edge until I could see the ice wall and swing at it with the hammer. I was hanging on to the ice axe, reaching to my side to place the hammer solidly into the wall with my left hand. I got it to bite after a few blows but wasn't happy about it and removed it to try again. I wanted it to be perfect before I removed the axe embedded in the lip and lowered myself on to the hammer. As the hammer came out there was a sharp cracking sound and my right hand, gripping the axe, pulled down. The sudden jerk turned me outwards and instantly I was falling.

I hit the slope at the base of the cliff before I saw it coming. I was facing into the slope and both knees locked as I struck it. I felt a shattering blow in my knee, felt bones splitting, and screamed. The impact catapulted me over backwards and down the slope of the East Face. I slid, head-first, on my back. The rushing speed of it confused me. I thought of the drop below but felt nothing. Simon would be ripped off the mountain. He couldn't hold this. I screamed again as I jerked to a sudden violent stop.

Everything was still, silent. My thoughts raced madly. Then pain flooded down my thigh – a fierce burning fire coming down the inside of my thigh, seeming to ball in my groin, building and building until I cried out at it, and my breathing came in ragged gasps. My leg! Oh Jesus. My leg!

I hung, head down, on my back, left leg tangled in the rope above me and my right leg hanging slackly to one side. I lifted my head from the snow and stared, up across my chest, at a grotesque distortion in the right knee, twisting the leg into a strange zigzag. I didn't connect it with the pain which burnt my groin. That had nothing to do with my knee. I kicked my left leg free of the rope and swung round until I was hanging against the snow on my chest, feet down. The pain eased. I kicked my left foot into the slope and stood up.

A wave of nausea surged over me. I pressed my face into the snow, and the sharp cold seemed to calm me. Something terrible, something dark with dread occurred to me, and as I thought about it I felt the dark thought break into panic: 'I've broken my leg, that's it. I'm dead. Everyone said it . . . if there's just two of you a broken ankle could turn into a death sentence . . . if it's broken . . . if . . . It doesn't hurt so much, maybe I've just ripped something.'

I kicked my right leg against the slope, feeling sure it wasn't broken. My knee exploded. Bone grated, and the fireball rushed from groin to knee. I screamed. I looked down at the knee and could see it was broken, yet I tried not to believe what I was seeing. It wasn't just broken, it was ruptured, twisted, crushed, and I could see the kink in the joint and knew what had happened. The impact had driven my lower leg up through the knee joint.

Oddly enough, looking at it seemed to help. I felt detached from it, as if I were making a clinical observation of someone else. I moved the knee gingerly, experimenting with it. I tried to bend it and stopped immediately, gasping at the rush of pain. When it moved I felt a grinding crunch; bone had moved, and a lot more besides. At least it wasn't an open fracture. I knew this as soon as I tried to move. I could feel no wetness, no blood. I reached down and caressed the knee with my right hand, trying to ignore the stabs of fire, so that I could feel it with enough force to be certain I wasn't bleeding. It was in one solid piece, but it felt huge, and twisted – and not mine. The pain kept flooding round it, pouring on fire, as if that might cure it then and there.

With a groan I squeezed my eyes tight shut. Hot tears filled my eyes, and my contact lenses swam in them. I squeezed tight again and felt hot drops rolling over my face. It wasn't the pain, I felt sorry for myself, childishly so, and with that thought I couldn't help the tears. Dying had seemed so far away, and yet now everything was tinged with it. I shook my head to stop the tears, but the taint was still there.

I dug my axes into the snow, and pounded my good leg deeply into the soft slope until I felt sure it wouldn't slip. The effort brought back the nausea and I felt my head spin giddily to the point of fainting. I moved and a searing spasm of pain cleared away the faintness. I could see the summit of Serie Norte away to the west. I was not far below it. The sight drove home how desperately things had changed. We were above 19,000 feet, still on the ridge, and very much alone. I looked south at the small rise I had hoped to scale quickly and it seemed to grow with every second that I stared. I would never get over it. Simon would not be able to get me up it. He would leave me. He had no choice. I held my breath, thinking about it. Left here? Alone? I felt cold at the thought. I remembered Rob, who had been left to die . . . but Rob had been unconscious, had been dying. I had only a bad leg. Nothing to kill me. For an age I felt overwhelmed at the notion of being left; I felt like screaming, and I felt like swearing, but stayed silent. If I said a word I would panic. I could feel myself teetering on the edge of it.

The rope which had been tight on my harness went slack. Simon was coming! He must know something had happened, I thought, but what shall I tell him? If I told him that I had only hurt my leg and not broken it, would that make him help me? My mind raced at the prospect of telling him that I was hurt. I pressed my face into the cold snow again and tried to think calmly. I had to cool it. If he saw me panicky and hysterical he might give up at once. I fought to stem my fears. Be rational about it, I thought. I felt myself calm down, and my breathing became steady; even the pain seemed tolerable.

'What happened? Are you OK?'

I looked up in surprise. I hadn't heard his approach. He stood at the top of the cliff looking down at me, puzzled. I made an effort to talk normally, as if nothing had happened:

'I fell. The edge gave way.' I paused, then I said as unemotionally as I could: 'I've broken my leg.'

His expression changed instantly. I could see a whole range of reactions in his face. I kept looking directly at him. I wanted to miss nothing.

'Are you sure it's broken?'

'Yes.'

He stared at me. It seemed that he looked harder and longer than he should have done because he turned away sharply. Not sharply enough though. I had seen the look come across his face briefly, but in that instant I knew his thoughts. He had an odd air of detachment. I felt unnerved by it, felt suddenly quite different from him, alienated. His eyes had been full of thoughts. Pity. Pity and something else; a distance given to a wounded animal which could not be helped. He had tried to hide it, but I had seen in, and I looked away full of dread and worry.

'I'll abseil down to you.'

He had his back to me, bending over a snow stake, digging down through the soft snow. He sounded matter-of-fact, and I wondered whether I was being unduly paranoid. I waited for him to say more, but he remained silent and I wondered what he was thinking. A short but very dangerous abseil from a poorly anchored snow stake put him down next to me quickly.

He stood close by me and said nothing. I had seen him glance at my leg but he made no comment. After some searching he found a packet of Paracetamols and handed me two pills. I swallowed them, and watched him trying to pull the abseil rope down. It refused to move. It had jammed in the snow bollard that he had dug around the snow stake above. Simon swore and set off towards the point where the wall was smallest, right on the crest of the ridge. I knew it was all unstable powder and so did he, but he had no choice. I looked away, unwilling to watch what I was sure would be a fatal fall down the West Face. Indirectly it would kill me as well, only a little more slowly.

Simon had said nothing about what he would do, and I had been nervous to prompt him. In an instant an uncrossable gap had come between us and we were no longer a team working together.

POSTSCRIPT: *Simon Yates attempted to rescue Joe Simpson, but a further accident forced him to abandon his injured climbing partner, whom he believed had died after falling into a crevasse. Miraculously, Simpson managed to struggle out and then hobble for four days to the base camp which Yates was about to abandon.*

# EUROPE

CHRIS DUFF

# ON CELTIC TIDES
## One Man's Journey around
## Ireland by Sea Kayak

I CROSSED LISCANNON BAY under a sky that promised rain. It was cold and damp, the kind of cold that didn't make sense for July. The water dripping off the shaft of the paddle was warm compared to the chill of the air. Ahead of me, massive waves rolled over a reef, lifting black and shiny, curling higher and steeper until whatever held the wave intact finally let loose and it collapsed in a deafening rumble of white. It was a crushing, terrifying power that re-formed, reaching around the ends of the reef and racing on to the cliff face I was paddling parallel to. I had landed for a quick break on a ledge beneath the cliffs, protected from the outer swell by this very reef. Now I was heading back out and thinking I should have stayed ashore. If it hadn't been for the rising tide, the ledge disappearing by the minute, I would have. Another swell rolled in, lifted as it raced over the shallows, and folded. Again and again the cycle repeated. Each time I was twenty yards closer to the reef and the headland above it. I changed course, angling away to deeper water.

I was watching for the rogue wave, the one in a thousand that was deeper, more deadly because it would break where no other wave would.

Veils of mist drifted below the cliffs, vapour from the thunder of the reef and the waves climbing twenty feet on to the cliff face. Beyond the rocks, the sea settled into the hypnotic rise and fall of deep water. The seaward side of the waves looked benign. That's what made it dangerous, to get lulled into the rhythm of the swells and wander too close. I paddled wide of the point, clear of any possible breaker, then turned and saw beyond the headland.

Hags Head was the beginning of a line of cliff broken by huge pieces of rock torn from the face, leaving caverns and sea stacks to stand alone against the ocean. In a jagged line, black against grey sky, the towers climbed, plummeted, and climbed again. Magnificent and dramatic in the weighted grey of the day, yet dwarfed by a mountainous wall of cliff that rose beyond and above them.

I had been anticipating this moment for days – my first glimpse of the Cliffs of Moher. The noise of the reef faded as I paddled around Hags Head and slowly drew closer to the cliffs. Over six hundred feet high, the single mass ran unbroken for three miles, bold and impenetrable as any fortress. Bands of white sedimentary rock separated fifty or sixty feet of darker layers, giving measure to the heights capped in green. Towers of rock, two hundred feet tall and bearing the same striations, stood cut off by the water, a geological indicator of where the cliffs had once reached further out to sea.

In the light rain, darkened skies and heavy swells, the visage of the cliffs was intimidating. I stayed a half mile offshore, wanting to be in closer, to look straight up the face of the cliff, but afraid of the confusion of rebounding waves at the base.

A swell lifted then lowered me into a trough that stole the bottom three hundred feet of the cliff from view. It rolled away toward the land and another cycle began, another onslaught of rolling energy gathering speed in the shallower waters around the towers, crashing in rings of white, then hitting the outermost points of the cliff. A split second apart, three faces of wall silently exploded. For a mile on either side, a line of white powered into the cliffs, hung for a second, then disappeared. Seconds later I heard a muffled rumble, another bank of wave approached the stacks, and the cycle of impact and sound confused my eye and ear.

I was chilled, the rain soaking through my hat and sending a shiver between my shoulders. I wanted to stay, watch one more cycle, but knew I had to get moving. The weather was changing fast and there was no place to land for the next five miles. Already the two outer Aran Islands were lost in cloud and rain. The third and closest was more shadow than land. With the front moving so rapidly, there would be wind – wind I didn't want to deal with. Suddenly there was a sense of urgency, fuelled by the energy of the cliffs and the approaching storm. Black on black: the water, cliffs and sky were one.

The paddle sliced into the swells, churned the water, and slowly the boat began to move. Four strokes, six, then eight. The bow wake surged with each pull. Running parallel with the swells the boat lifted with each wave, two strokes on the crest, then dropping sideways into the trough for another two. Back up on the shoulder, over the top for a quick look around, then rolling into the trough again. The slight burning in my shoulders faded as I warmed to the pace and the automatic movements of my body took over. Toes, knees and hips were the contact points, relaxed yet firmly planted while the rotation of upper body, stomach, back and shoulders did most of the work.

The paddle shaft flexed, pulled against fingers, and released as one blade leaped out of the water and the opposite one dove in. Moments would pass and I was lost in the magic of reaching and pulling, feeling the blending of storm, swell, mind and body becoming one. The threat of being caught out on the open water by the storm had been the impetus for the charge of energy running through me. On the crests was the point of land I was heading for. Reach and pull, storm darkness overhead. Wind waves started to cover the swells and grabbed the paddle in warning. I was barely ahead of the storm, engrossed in the moment, trying to win the race and at the same time almost hoping it would catch me.

As the first rain drilled into the deck, I paddled into Doolin Harbour and dragged the boat up between some boulders. Sea to land, the transition was always so sudden. The sky opened up with fat cold drops. Thoughts of the last hours of paddling were pushed aside and the immediate concern of finding a place to camp took over. The only level, dry ground was a tourist campground three hundred yards from the high water mark.

On the first trip I set up the tent, the priority, to keep the gear as dry as possible during the unloading. Three more trips around boulders and great slabs of rock that teetered with each misplaced step and I was exhausted. The air was filled with the sound of heavy rain drops, sheets of it that splattered on rock and harbour. I tasted the salt washed from my face and felt the rivulets running over my hands and dripping from each finger. Empty of energy from the race with the storm and the trips up and down the beach, I stood and looked at the boat. I dreaded this part, lifting the seventy pounds of boat and gear and carrying it over the rocks. One wrong step and the weight of the boat balanced on my shoulder would drive us hard into the rocks. Broken fibreglass, broken bones. I pushed the thought away.

There was no use standing in the downpour and thinking about it. I turned and reached for the cockpit combing, and paused. Two guys were heading my way through the rain-slicked rocks. They had seen me coming over the rocks with bags of food and gear, then disappearing for another load. Fortunately for me, they were kayakers and knew the hassle of trying to carry a boat solo. After a quick introduction we split the last of the gear and carried the boat through the rock maze.

Marty and Garth were on a weekend break from jobs in the North. They had gotten rained out on a rock climb and were camped, waiting for a break in the weather. They wanted to hear about the trip and offered a ride to the pub a mile into town. I threw the last of the gear into the tent, tied the boat to the windward side, and piled into their car beside packs, ropes and climbing hardware.

The pub was crammed with people escaping the rain – Germans, Americans, Japanese and Irish. People milling in a blur of coloured raingear and wet heads. Everyone smiling, ordering rounds of Guinness, and crowding tighter around the tables when another friend came in dripping wet.

We found a table against the back wall, ordered fish and chips and a beer each, then settled into talk of sea kayaking, river paddling and climbing. We talked about stretches of the coast we had all paddled, how the rock formations and caves had looked, and where we had camped. I asked if they knew Jim Kennedy, a paddler I had met on a dock in Schull, County Cork. Sure enough, they knew him; in a country as small as Ireland and a sport as tightly knit as sea paddling, everyone seemed to know everyone else.

KATHERINE KIZILOS

# THE OLIVE GROVE
## Travels in Greece

N AZIF DROVE US back to Komotini, full of apologies for the
shabbiness of his car. On the way, he pointed out the river
where he and Fedai had gone fishing together and the neighbouring village where his wife had been born. The late afternoon sky
was enormous, the clouds billowing impressively as though to
compensate for the meandering flatness of the plain, the bewildering sameness of the fields.

As we approached the town, Nazif quietly remarked: 'A white
car has been following us for a while. It is probably the police.'

Bill and I looked behind us in alarm. Neither of us had noticed
the small white car. As Nazif double-parked in the square outside
our hotel, the white car pulled up behind us. Nazif said he had first
noticed it when we had driven by his wife's village; it was therefore
possible that the police had been discreetly monitoring our movements all afternoon. Bill and I stared in disbelief as two casually
dressed men got out of the car and sauntered towards a kiosk on the
corner of the square. Then the driver of the white car pulled away.

'They just want to scare you,' said Nazif.

'Well, they've succeeded.'

Nazif allowed himself a small smile at our expense. 'You don't
have anything to worry about,' he said. 'The worst they can do is
take you to the station for questioning.'

It was hardly a comforting remark, but Nazif's intentions were
good. We thanked him, and he told us to phone if we needed any
help. Then he too drove away.

Our first impulse was to check our hotel room to see if it had been searched in our absence. It appeared to be untouched. Before we went out again, however, I took two snapshots of my son from a folder in my case and put them in my wallet; I had a superstitious dread of strangers handling the photographs. As we walked back through the lobby I saw one of the men from the white car leaving the hotel. I remembered an odd occurrence that had taken place the day before, when we were lunching at a small restaurant near the centre of Komotini. Halfway through our meal, the waiter had asked me if my name was Katerina: I was wanted on the telephone. I'd felt a small jolt of fear. None of our acquaintances knew our whereabouts. 'Maybe we are being followed,' I'd joked to Bill. But as it turned out, the caller was chasing someone else with the same name. We'd chuckled at the coincidence and he'd apologised for disturbing me.

'*Koppelia* – Girlie!' The hotel receptionist, a woman of my own age with peroxided hair and an annoyingly patronising manner, was calling me. Did I have ID?

'Why do you want it? We already showed our ID when we checked in.'

'We have his ID' – and here she nodded towards Bill – 'but we haven't seen yours.'

'But that's not unusual, is it? Usually one ID is enough.'

She didn't answer but held out her hand for the passport. Irritated, I waited as she took down my particulars. What was this about? Had someone asked her for my ID? I guessed that she wouldn't answer my questions, so I didn't ask them.

When the receptionist had finished, Bill and I walked across the square to a cafe and ordered a pizza. It was late afternoon; we hadn't eaten a proper meal since breakfast. The restaurant was decorated in a flash modern style to attract moneyed students from the university; rock and roll thudded out with a dull inevitability. We went upstairs to escape the noise and sat near the window, looking down at the two men from the white car as they paced up and down. Occasionally they looked back up at us.

'This is ridiculous,' said Bill. 'These guys are so obvious.'

'Well, if the idea is to scare us, it's their job to be obvious.'

Bill told me of a cousin of ours, now a magistrate, who had been followed by the police while she was a law student in Komotini. The reason, she believed, was that she had befriended some Turkish students. We supposed that we had attracted attention by visiting Ismail Rodoplu, a Turk who had represented Thrace in the Greek Parliament. We had talked to Rodoplu – a hearty, red-haired fellow – in his office that morning. The scene had recalled the smoky, conspiratorial atmosphere of a village *kafeneion*, with its perpetual crowd of gossips, intriguers and hangers-on. A boy was summoned to fetch a tray loaded with coffee and iced water from a nearby shop; meanwhile a knot of Turkish men walked in and out of the office, whispering, listening, drinking coffee and occasionally joining in. A Turkish lawyer interrupted from time to time to clear up ambiguities in Rodoplu's Greek. Rodoplu was concerned that no Turks had been compensated for damages incurred during the Komotini riots of 1990, when a Greek crowd had smashed and looted Turkish shops and businesses, including his electoral office. Apparently, only a small proportion of the Turks affected had filed for compensation; they were too frightened to make a legal protest and had little confidence in the system.

Our pizza arrived: vegetarian with chilli. I picked up a piece and peered down at the men from the white car. They were smoking and looking bored. I thought about how terrible I would feel if this surveillance led to a stamp in my passport denying me entry back into Greece, and I asked Bill to ring our cousin the magistrate for advice. She told him not to worry: she did not believe the police would search our room, or even call us in for questioning. We had done nothing wrong. 'They just want to scare you,' she said.

'This really isn't so bad,' said Bill, putting away his mobile phone. 'It's all good material. After this I'll be able to write about what it feels like to be followed. I might include a little episode like this in my next book.'

'And how do you feel? What will you say?'

He thought about it for a moment and looked down again at the two men in the square. 'That it makes you paranoid – but if you eat a pizza you feel better.'

That evening we went to the movies and saw an execrable action film involving fast cars, gun fights, explosions, mistaken identity and a vegetarian girl in a mini-skirt. When we returned to our hotel room the phone was ringing. I picked up the receiver, but no one was there.

An army band woke us early the next morning, our last in Komotini. It was rehearsing the national anthem for the Ohi (or 'No') march that was to take place in every main street in Greece later that day. I stepped onto our balcony, with its Arabian Nights view of a minaret silhouetted against the distant hills, and glanced down at the soldiers. They looked rather comical, like khaki-coloured wind-up toys. Their routine involved turning corners, apparently at random, while blowing bugles and banging drums. I wondered out loud if we would arrive at Xanthi – our next stop – in time for the march. Bill made a dry remark about the noisy intrusion of ill-timed nationalism; hadn't I seen enough of that already? He was opposed, on principle, to all patriotic display.

Before checking out we breakfasted at a modest little *bougatsa* shop on the other side of the square. As far as possible, I was following a *bougatsa*-a-day policy while in northern Greece. The best places were unpretentious, with lino floors and steamy windows; they only served three or four varieties of the filo-pastry pies (custard, cheese, spinach and mince were the standards), and were open early in the morning. Many did not have chairs or tables; you took the *bougatsa* away, wrapped up in paper, or maybe ate it standing at the counter. On this morning, Bill bought an extra one for an Albanian child whom we had seen every day, begging for coins. The woman in the shop smiled at Bill but glared at the child; she didn't want him hanging around. The dark-haired boy was dressed in clothes that were too thin, and his face was unwashed. He murmured thanks, grabbed the slightly greasy parcel and ran away.

We saw illegal refugees from Albania's collapsed Hoxha regime in every town through which we passed. They were, for the most part, beggars and scapegoats, accused of petty theft and of making the streets unsafe: a real indictment in a country that has always prided itself on the civility of its urban life. On a social level, Albanians were barely tolerated. Complaints about their shiftlessness were as common as conversations about the weather. But they were also widely employed as casual labourers because they would work for half the daily rate paid to Greeks. It was an inconsistency that few Greeks were prepared to acknowledge.

'*Kaki anthropi*,' said the woman in the *bougatsa* shop, gesturing towards the fleeing boy. 'Bad people.'

'This place is full of people who don't like each other,' said Bill as we walked back to the hotel. He offered to bring our bags down to the foyer while I settled the bill. The bottle blonde was at the desk again. Without looking up, she charged me 2500 drachmas more for the room than we had negotiated.

'You've made a mistake,' I said.

'Maybe you just didn't understand my girl.'

'I don't think so . . .'

Bill arrived with the bags. He was the one who had arranged the price for the room, so I explained the problem to him. The blonde was now openly agitated. She asked him to describe the receptionist he had dealt with.

Bill shrugged. 'It was a man . . .'

'That's impossible. No man was working when you checked in. You're lying. That's the second lie you've told me.'

Her raised voice was filled with hatred. The conflict over the bill was merely the hook for her anger, not its underlying cause.

Bill picked up our bags and cocked his head towards the door. 'Let's get out of here.'

A man emerged from the office behind the desk. Steadily, quietly, he told the receptionist to accept the price Bill had agreed to pay. Relieved by his intervention, I counted out the drachma notes. Nobody spoke. But as we walked through the door, the blonde was unable to resist shouting a final farewell: 'You'll be arrested one day!'

BRIAN HALL

# STEALING FROM A DEEP PLACE
## Travels in Southeastern Europe

OUT OF THE DARKEST blue came the sound of hooves, the slap of reins. I was instantly wide awake. I zipped open the top of the tent and sat up. The trees around me were black and the glimmering light of dawn had not yet gathered at one side of the sky. From the road, thirty yards away, I caught a flicker of movement. A creaking of trees in the wind drifted along the ground – but there was no wind.

I got out of the tent and threw on some clothes. I picked my way through the spruce trees, toward the road. A black shape crossed the opening in the trees. I hung back, in the shadows, where I could not be seen.

The shape of a wagon passed by, groaning over the rocks. The horse slipped in the dew on the uneven ground. The silhouette of a boy sat on the perch, chin tucked, toes curled around the footrest; a tree branch to beat the horse with curved up and out beside him like a black fountain, frozen. The wagon was piled high with shadows, outlines of rough and worn-out necessities. Two men followed, leading a horse mounted with sacks. Then women, trailing their skirts in the wet dirt, and accompanying their movement with a labial, tuneful muttering. Another man, wearing theatrical spurs. A woman, and a child whining mechanically, like a dog. Now and then, louder words by the men floating up and down the line. Twenty people in the darkness, heading east.

It was six o'clock. The Gypsies were on the move.

I stood still. The mongrels came last, gliding with the furtiveness of weasels from side to side of the lane, their tails permanently down. They didn't smell me, about which I was very glad. When it was totally silent again, the eastern edge of the sky was aquamarine.

I had seen no bears, no wolves, no vipers that night. There were probably few of the first, and none of the second any longer in the Carpathians, despite what the Hungarians had said. The wolves used to kill people, but more importantly, they used to kill sheep – and they were hunted as pests, for rewards. The bears were not as dangerous, or as disruptive, as the wolves. The Gypsies used to catch and tame the bears, pull out their teeth and claws, and teach them to 'dance' by forcing them to walk on hot metal sheets while they fiddled a certain tune. Bears are as intelligent as dogs, and after several repetitions of this, the bear would 'dance', from the memory of exquisite pain, whenever the tune was played. And so the bear would perform for the *gadjé* – the sedentary village folk, whom the Gypsies despised. The gadjé never lost their fascination for dancing bears, and they would applaud in delight while the Gypsy women moved in the crowd and deftly picked their pockets. Who could blame the Gypsies for despising such rubes?

But the bears were gone now, and the Gypsies had long since run out of gullible villagers. Their rackets had worked when Europe was large, when they could flee one outraged town in the direction of another, unsuspecting one. There had been no such thing, in either the fourteenth century or the nineteenth, as a country with guard towers and fences all the way around it. In modern Romania, the Gypsies were trapped, and the system was waiting for them. Ceauşescu's government had made it clear that they would have to learn, sooner or later, how to be socialist citizens.

Sunlight flamed the tips of the spruce trees as I rolled up my tent and stuffed it in with the sleeping bag. I carried the bike out to the dirt road and pointed it after the Gypsies. There was little chance that I would catch up with them. The bike, on this rocky, sandy path, would be even slower than the Gypsies' wooden, springless wagons. I started off, the line of tree shadows pointing toward me like the planted spears of a line of defence.

The road grew worse, and I progressed that morning at a crawl.

Then a spoke broke, and I spent an hour in the shade of a sycamore, with the bike on its back and the rear wheel in pieces. I reached Faget just before noon and realised I had gone only eighteen kilometres.

Faget was a large, bustling village, on the important road from Lugoj to Deva. Yet none of the streets was paved, and the village seemed to be drowning in dust. The sand at the main crossroads came up to my ankles. Bicycles do not work under those conditions, and I pushed the thing, slipping and sliding, from one corner to the next. People stopped and stared.

'Changemoney?'

*'Nu – va rog.'*

'Hey – Marlboro?'

*'Scusi – ma non fumo.'*

They walked next to me, and I kept pushing. They tried to catch my eye and spoke encouragingly. I was willing to talk, but they didn't want talk. I couldn't help them. Eventually, they peeled off. I got water from a fountain at the railway station. I pushed some more.

I saw, for the first time, an *alimentari* that was open, and I went in. But in the forty-watt gloom inside, the shelves were nearly empty. I asked for bread, but the sharp-faced woman behind the counter shook her head. At her back, on the plain wooden shelves, were a few old tubes of mustard, label-less jars filled with a dark, greasy compound, and a set of small cardboard boxes (salt?), each fronted with a drawing of a smiling child. There was nothing else.

The pavement came back on the far side of Faget. Now there was a headwind, but I made better progress. Under a cloudless sky, I followed a line of poplars – supple trees, holding their arms high and swaying – for several miles.

The village of Coşava had a pretty square, with benches bolted down between clipped bushes and a modern sculpture pretending to be the centre of attention. No one accosted me at first, and I risked sitting in the square to eat my lunch. I had barely begun, when a very small man with fly-blown, greying hair trotted up to me and spoke excitedly in German:

'This is great! This is great! I can't believe this! Where are you coming from?'

'Uh . . . America –'

'America?! I can't believe that! Incredible! Tell me, what would you like?'

'Excuse me?'

'Don't you want anything? Some food, perhaps? Something to drink? Come, I'll get you a beer.'

Whenever I am trying to get my bearings, I tend to repeat people. So I said, 'A beer?'

'What, you don't like beer? Fine! I can get you something else. What would you like? Chocolate?' The man never stopped moving. He walked to one end of the bench and back, clapped his hands, waved his arms when he spoke to me.

'Chocolate?' I said, watching him go from side to side. He placed his hands on his lower back and leaned far backward, stretching. Then he tipped forward and paced, bent over. He repeated both motions.

If he knew where to get food, I was interested. But I wanted to figure out how strange he was first.

He poked at the bike. 'Amazing. Just amazing.' He pointed to things. 'Sleeping bag, tyre pump, water bottle, bags, hey – dirty clothes, here, in the net – great, great! Very smart. I have done this, too, you know.'

'Oh?'

'I used to go 200 kilometres a day, 250.' He started to touch his toes, very rapidly. 'I stretched out like this, first. Then I went everywhere: 260, 70 kilometres a day. I have gone by bicycle all over these mountains. I was born in Szaszsebes.'

Szaszsebes. The Hungarian name for Sebeş. Now I knew why he spoke good German. The man was a Magyar.

'I don't do it any more, because my back is no good. Now I walk instead. The bicycle' – he waggled a finger admonishingly – 'too much bending.' He bent over and touched his toes again. 'No, this kind of bending is good! But that other kind' – he shook his head – '*szonyü* – horrible.'

He was the first Magyar I had met in Romania. When the new border was drawn between Hungary and Romania in 1920, the area around the Arad district was so intermixed that the ethnologists at the Paris Conference had despaired of finding a dividing line. Arad itself was one-third Magyar. But now, in 1982, I had met no Magyars, heard no Hungarian. Did that mean there were fewer of them? Had they moved to cities with old Hungarian majorities, like Kolozsvár? Had they been moved by the authorities? Perhaps they were still here in southern Transylvania, only hidden. The Hungarians in Budapest had told me that the Magyars in Transylvania were afraid to go out in the streets, that they only looked out through cracks in their shutters.

How true was any of this? Here was someone to ask.

'You're a Magyar,' I said.

He gave me a quick look. 'Yes.'

But it would never get beyond that. As I stood up, a couple of other men were walking toward us. They were not at all menacing. It looked as if they had noticed my bicycle from across the street and were coming out of curiosity.

But the little man whipped around and said to them, 'Get back! Get back!' He placed himself between the men and my bike.

The two men smiled. They appeared to recognise the Magyar. They spoke to him in Romanian.

'Stay away!' the Magyar yelled, in German. 'Don't touch it!' He looked over his shoulder at me and said urgently, 'Let's go.'

Two or three others were approaching, from the opposite direction. They, too, seemed to be just curious, attracted by the bike and the excited little man. One of them called out a question to me, in Romanian. Something about where I was headed.

But the Magyar stopped me from answering. 'Don't talk to these pigs,' he said. And then to them: 'Get away! Stand back!' And then something vituperative in Romanian.

Everyone seemed to know the man. They were not surprised at his behaviour. They came closer, to see the bike. One of them reached out a hand; he was about to speak.

But the Magyar jumped and pushed him back violently. He

bellowed now in Romanian, a long string of abuse, then the German word *schwein*. The man who was pushed tried to retreat and bumped into another man; there was a confusion of arms. Another Romanian tried to hold the Magyar down, but he squirmed out of his grasp and swung wildly at the man's face. The spectators on the opposite side of the ring – we were in a ring now, the Magyar and I – kept smiling. Apparently none of this, not even the punching, was unusual. But the smiles showed a measure of exasperation. The Romanians might lose their tempers at some point.

The Magyar turned to me, grabbed my arm roughly. He said in a loud voice, 'Let's go, let's go! They'll steal something.' And to the Romanians – 'Leave him alone!' I thought he was going to add, 'He's mine!' Then suddenly he dropped my arm and flew behind me, barrelling into another Romanian. 'Get back!' The Romanian almost fell over, and a look of real anger came over his face.

The situation had ceased to make any sense to me, and I wanted no part of it. I jammed my lunch hurriedly into my knapsack, grabbed the bike, and excused myself, to no one in particular. I stepped away from the centre. To my relief, the ring broke for me. The Romanians were more interested in the little man now than in a foreign cyclist. I feared the Magyar would grab me from behind, but he didn't. I kept walking, without looking back. The sounds of cursing retreated. I could hear the Magyar's rasping voice and the basso shouts of the Romanians. At the edge of the square, I climbed on the bike and pedalled out of Coşava.

Two kilometres down the road, I stopped again to eat lunch at a road marker, where I could sit against the stone and be out of the wind. Two boys showed up while I was eating and pestered me for cigarettes. I was not entirely kind to them, and I felt bad about it afterward.

# ASIA

MARIA COFFEY

# A BOAT IN OUR BAGGAGE
## Around the World with a Kayak

WHILE DAG STILL SLEPT, I crawled out of the tent. In the dawn light the river looked like dull pewter, and tendrils of mist crept along its surface. Quickly, I undressed, and despite my only companions being two red-legged storks delicately stepping across a nearby sandbar, I wrapped myself in a length of cloth. I'd learned that in India people can materialise from nowhere, and to be found bathing naked in the Ganga would be an untenable transgression of holy law. As I waded into the sluggish water, the storks flapped their wings and skimmed away with long legs trailing behind them. Holding my nose, I immersed myself for three quick, cold dips, then struggled back to the bank. Bending to my small pile of clothes, I realised I was standing among cinders and brittle bone fragments. Nearby, a makeshift stretcher and a muddy shroud lay discarded.

After three weeks on the river, we'd grown used to seeing cremations in all their various stages. We'd seen naked corpses being ceremonially smeared with ghee, we'd seen a man carrying a lighted torch five times around the pyre on which his dead father lay, we'd seen people too poor to afford enough fuel simply pushing a half-burned body into the water. Later that day, as we paddled by the third cremation in as many hours, Dag and Bapi lapsed into black humour.

'Smells like chicken – must have been a skinny one.'

'No, no, you are quite wrong, it is smelling exactly like roast beef. This was a fatter person!'

As always, the mourners ran to the water's edge, beckoning to us. We didn't intend to stop. We wanted to reach Fatehgarh that day, and we had no clear idea of the distance we had to cover.

'You will get there by nightfall,' a sadhu we'd met earlier had predicted.

'It's fifty kilometres away,' a fisherman standing waist-deep in the river had told us. Now, the mourners had yet another estimate.

*'Do sau kilomitar!'* they cried. 'Two hundred kilometres! Come and rest!'

We put our palms together in *namaskar* and carried on. After a few paddle strokes, I turned to wave at the men. They were shading their eyes with their hands to watch our departure. Seen through the flame-heated air, they appeared to shimmer, like ghostly creatures. The river took a wide bend, and suddenly the men were out of sight.

The next section of the river had a forsaken feeling to it. It made tortuous loops, a hot searing wind swept across the plain and the sky glared down. There was nothing to distract us from the monotony save sandbanks and skeletons. Once, we became stranded on a bank in the company of a full human skeleton, picked clean of flesh but with cloth still wrapped around its torso.

We'd already given up the idea of trying to reach Fatehgarh that day when we saw a red flag fluttering from a long pole, the sign of an encampment of sadhus. Drifting toward us on the wind were the rhythmic beating of a gong and the droning of a mantra: 'Sita Ram Sita Ram Sita Ram Sita Ram . . .'A crowd of sadhus ran down to the riverbank and pulled our boats ashore. They had long matted hair and were ash-smeared and naked except for loin-cloths. Around their feet, scabby, dun-coloured dogs barked, leaped and fought, raising clouds of sand. The sadhus told us they were camped here for the month of Magh with their 111-year-old guru, Moni Baba. Chattering excitedly, they led us to a large tent made of ragged canvas thrown over bamboo poles. Next to it, some women from the nearby village of Kadarga were sitting in the dirt making rotis and potato sabzee. They stopped working to stare at us, and the cloud of flies buzzing around them settled on to the dough, changing its pasty grey colour to black.

Inside the tent, the ground was spread with dusty straw and the air was thick with flies, but it was a welcome respite from the wind and the blinding light outside. We were brought mugs of lukewarm tea that was the same muddy colour as the river. Several sadhus crouched around to watch us drink it. Others peered around the tent flap and through holes in the canvas. Despite my strong suspicion that the water hadn't been boiled, I gulped it down. The sadhus grinned in delight. The tent flap was thrown back and a young sadhu came in with two plates heaped with sabzee and rotis. Fleetingly, I remembered the fly-covered dough outside, and then I pushed the thought aside.

'They are asking us to sleep tonight in this tent,' said Bapi.

I looked doubtfully at the thick cloud of flies circling our heads. The sadhus' eyes followed mine.

'They are telling,' said Bapi, 'that you must not worry about these flies, because when darkness comes they will go home.'

Bowls of warm buffalo milk and lumps of gur followed next. To allay the arrival of yet more food, we requested an audience with Moni Baba.

We were ushered to the doorway of a tiny tent. Two sadhus knelt either side of a heap of blankets and began singing to it. The heap stirred. A hand emerged. The blankets were thrown back and a wizened old man sat up. His rheumy eyes were heavily lidded and his head was totally bald except for a few long strands of fine hair sprouting from the crown. He was instantly alert and listened carefully to the sadhus' explanation of who we were and what we were doing. Then, as this was his weekly day of silence, he reached for a chalkboard. While he scrawled some Hindi script, I noticed how remarkably young his hands looked. Bapi translated what he wrote.

'Moni Baba says that our yatra purifies the food we eat and the water we drink.'

With a measure of relief, I thought of the meal we'd just consumed.

'He says that we will reach Varanasi in safety, but the hardest part of the journey is ahead. He says that we should sing *Rama Sita*.'

The guru began clapping his hands together. Feeling rather self-conscious, we chanted the mantra in time with him. The sadhus pressing around the tent joined in, the man beating the gong fell into our rhythm, conches were blown, cymbals clashed and soon the entire camp echoed with fervent singing. Despite the heat inside the tent, and the flies crawling over my face and arms, I felt myself slipping into a strange, hypnotic state, and I gazed in homage at the old man before me. Abruptly, he held up his hands for silence. All around the camp, the singing and music faded away. He closed his eyes, and his lips moved as if in prayer. There was a pregnant hush in and around the tent. Then the guru's heavy lids snapped open, and his eyes twinkled at Dag.

'Good day, sir!' he cried, and dissolved into helpless chuckling.

The sadhus gasped in alarm: the guru had broken his day of silence!

Moni Baba composed himself.

'Today I go to Varanasi,' he solemnly pronounced. 'Yesterday, I went to Varanasi. Tomorrow I shall go to Varanasi.'

'He is practising his English!' cried Bapi.

The guru sneezed.

'Rama!' yelled the sadhus in unison. 'Sita Ram!' A fresh round of chanting and clapping ensued.

When darkness came, the flies did go home, forming a dense coating on the inside walls and ceiling of the tent. I lay in our sleeping bag, listening to the muttering of mantras all around the camp and wondering if Moni Baba had been right about the purification of our food. Since leaving Hardwar, every night I'd expected to wake up with the gut-wrenching pains that presage an attack of gastroenteritis. So far, though, I'd had the opposite problem: whether it was because of the starchy diet, or as a result of my inhibitions due to the lack of privacy and toilet paper, I was suffering, on the Ganges of all places, from constipation.

At six o'clock the flies woke and descended upon us, forcing us to flee the tent. All around the camp, sadhus were meditating, or doing puja at the water's edge, or hunkered around small fires. Moni Baba's appearance at eight drew them all together, and they greeted him with fervent delight, blowing on conches, banging on cymbals, gongs, drums and tin plates, and shouting out mantras. He shuffled along to a small platform shaded with yellow cloth, where he was lifted up to sit amid heaps of flowers, tin boxes filled with blessed sweets, pictures of Rama and holy books bound in red cloth. One by one the sadhus knelt before him to receive his blessing and accept a prasad of sweets. Then it was our turn. We strewed marigolds over his head and touched our foreheads to his feet. As he gave us prasad, he spoke in a childish, singsong voice.

Bapi's face broke into a huge grin. 'Moni Baba is wanting to see your kayak!'

Helped by the sadhus, the guru inched his way to the riverbank. For several minutes he stood in silence, staring down at the red boat. When he finally spoke his words were greeted with gasps and squeals of surprise.

'He is wanting to ride in the boat!' cried Bapi.

'Rama Sita!' the sadhus shouted. 'Sita Ram!'

I held the boat steady as the old man was lowered into the front cockpit. He pulled his shawl tightly around his shoulders, and held out one hand for his staff, which he laid across the deck. Dag got into the back of the kayak, tentatively pushed off from the bank and paddled the frail guru around in circles.

'Sita Ram, Sita Ram!' sang the sadhus, leaping about in pure joy and showering the boat with marigold heads.

'If you insist on these tearful leave-takings, you'd better learn how to blow your nose the Indian way,' said Dag as we paddled away from the camp.

Overcome by the exuberant faith of the sadhus, and by their

open-hearted acceptance of us, I was openly weeping. By the time I managed to stop the flood of tears, their chanting had faded out of earshot, and the marigold heads on the kayak deck were withering in the sun.

The river still lazily wound about, and despite long days of paddling we seemed to get no closer to Fatehgarh. But there was a change of atmosphere along the riverbanks. The curiosity of the farmers we met along the way was tinged with suspicion and resentment, and the warnings of dacoits steadily increased.

'There are jungle people around here,' the farmers said. 'You must not camp alone.'

We finally reached the outskirts of Fatehgarh on a bright and sunny morning. Women in vivid saris worked in fields of pumpkins and mustard, and dhobi wallahs stood in the river, wrestling with huge lengths of material which stained the water with red and purple dyes. All over the bank, shirts, saris and bolts of cotton were spread out to dry in the afternoon sun. Burros lay in the dirt, curled up and sleeping like dogs.

'To your left,' said Dag.

I looked, and wished I hadn't. A few feet away from us, the corpse of a young man floated on its side in a foetal position. The bloated skin was a sickly yellow colour, and part of the face was eaten away. During four weeks on the Ganges, my stomach had hardened up enough to withstand fly-infested food and water straight from the river, but this was simply too much for it.

'Are you OK?' asked Dag, when I stopped retching. 'Because there's another one up ahead.'

During the next twenty minutes, we paddled past a dozen more bodies. The fresher ones were still wrapped in cloth which ballooned up above the surface of the water. From a distance, they could have been mistaken for discarded pillowcases, were it not for the crows and vultures which flapped down to peck at them and the dogs which swam out for a meal. One of the bodies was tragically comical, floating face down with only the buttocks showing above the water. Another lay trapped on a sandbank, its ribcage exposed and pieces of its flesh fluttering in the current.

But worst of all was the corpse which had become completely submerged save for the feet: toes splayed, skin mottled and shrunken, and murky water concealing the horror below. This was the stuff of nightmares.

It was enough for one day. We went ashore at the ghats of a small temple, and the pujari hurried down to meet us.

'You are making a thesis about this river?' he shouted, standing a mere two feet away.

'Yes, we're collecting material for a book,' I replied.

'Very good! Very good! You are a poet?'

I told him I wasn't, and he shook his head as if in consolation.

'Oh dear. I am very sorry. Here in India, we like poets very much. What is the difference between India and your country?'

A corpse floated by; downstream, dogs fought over another that lay rotting on the bank.

'India is spiritual,' I said. 'My country is materialistic.'

'Ah, yes,' he responded. 'I have been hearing this before. Where is God?'

'God is everywhere,' I replied.

'It is true!' he cried, clapping his hands. 'Perhaps your husband is Lord Rama and you are his wife, Sita! So we treat you as our gods! You must sleep here tonight! There are many robbers close by but have no fear, we will be guarding you.'

Leaving the kayaks in his care, we walked into Fatehgarh. As we stopped off at street stalls to buy fruit, tea and rice, people pressed in at our backs and elbows, making it difficult for us to move. By the time we arrived at the post office, from where I wanted to place a call to my mother, the crowd had grown and practically filled the small room, where an ill-tempered clerk sat behind a desk.

'What is the code number for England?' I asked him.

Impatiently, he paged through a battered, torn telephone directory.

'You've gone past it,' I told him.

He slammed the book shut. 'The international section is missing!' he shouted. 'You must call from Varanasi!'

'I won't be there for two weeks,' I protested. 'Can't you call the operator?'

'The operator has gone!' he shouted.

'It's very important that I talk to my mother,' I coaxed. 'Please show me the directory.'

Reluctantly, he handed it over. Within seconds, I had located the international section and the country code for England. The clerk passed me an ancient black telephone, and I dialled my mother's number. There were whooshing and fizzing noises on the line, as if I was trying to connect with outer space, then a clear ringing began. On either side of me were men with their faces about three inches away from mine, and their eyes popping with curiosity.

'Hello, Mum,' I said, when she answered. 'I'm calling from a small town along the Ganges.'

'She is calling her mother,' announced the clerk to the crowd. 'Her mother is living in England. She is happy to be hearing from her daughter.'

'How are you?' asked my mother. 'What on earth is it like over there?'

'We're both really healthy,' I said. 'And it's incredible here, it's heartbreaking, inspiring, everything you can and can't imagine.'

Frowning, the clerk scratched his head. 'She is telling her mother how is the weather!' he triumphantly announced to the expectant crowd.

'What are you laughing about?' asked my mother.

STUART STEVENS

# NIGHT TRAIN TO TURKISTAN
## Modern Adventures along China's Ancient Silk Road

I T WAS SOMEWHERE around mid-morning, when we'd been on the road for four or five hours and the sun was just coming up, that I realised what I was travelling in was not so much a bus but a frozen toilet on wheels.

This thought came to me right after a bump had tossed me out of my seat on to the floor. I landed in a mixture of vomit and baby urine. The young mother across from me looked down sympathetically and offered her tiny hand, a friendly gesture aborted suddenly by another attack of the nausea she'd been struggling with all morning. She leaned sideways and retched at my feet. We hit another bump and the seat cushions – a generous classification – flew up all around me like pancakes tossed on a griddle.

I remembered, like scenes from another life, the outrage I would routinely express at airport counters whenever forced to take the centre seat on a plane. 'You don't have an aisle? You really expect me to . . .'

At 6 am, in the station at Daheyon, the bus hadn't looked so bad. With my increasingly sophisticated eye, I'd noticed immediately that the seats had solid backs, not the hollow kind that guaranteed you'd be riding all day with someone's knees jammed in your back. And though it didn't have heat, it also lacked the branding iron along the baseboard. One less life-threatening obstacle.

There was a tremendous crowd squeezed into the square cement box that served as a station. Mark, Fran and I elected to wait outside in front of the bus door, braced for the hand-to-hand

195

seating struggle. In one great rush, the crowd poured out of the station – and on to the bus next to ours. After checking that we had the right bus, we were elated. We pulled out of the station with a scraggly group filling only half the seats.

In a celebration of the unexpected room, I stretched out on the back row of seats and tried to sleep. I soon realised it was like trying to doze in a refrigerated washing machine. Not only did the bus lack heat, all the windows were broken or severely cracked. I tried to light a match to read my thermometer but it was impossible in the brisk cross-breeze.

The bus vibrated continuously, interspersed with violent bumps. In the dimness, I watched a baby shoot upward out of his mother's arms to be caught by his father. The little scene had the disastrous potential and happy ending of a well-rehearsed vaudeville act.

I wore: a layer of thin long underwear; another layer of thicker long underwear made from a miracle material called capeline; heavy wool pants; a wool shirt; a down vest; an expedition parka; my PLA flap hat; and ski gloves. My feet were wrapped in two Patagonia synchilla hats in addition to thick socks and boots.

I ran through this list in my head because I was cold and wondered what else I could put on. But I was wearing almost everything I had brought to China.

There was only one thing to do. I pulled out my sleeping bag and crawled in. The young mothers, seeing me in what looked like a giant baby snuggler, looked at me jealously. Even the woman who had been retching stopped and reached out imploringly, holding out her baby as if she wanted me to slip it inside the bag with me.

I declined.

The sun came up with a primeval, first-dawn quality I had begun to expect in desert China. There was an intimidating line of peaks to the south and brown wasteland ahead. The interior of the bus had been painted green a long time ago; a silly fringe of dirty cloth hung from the ceiling, as if a decorator had once tried to create a romantic surrey feel for the conveyance.

At the very front of the bus, the official team of driver, female conductor and travelling mechanic rode in a separate compartment divided by a door of broken glass. This little section appeared heated, and there was no vomit or urine on the floor. I viewed it enviously as a first-class haven and wondered what matter of bribe or enticement – I was up for anything – it might take to gain entrance.

The ride to Kashgar from Turpan cost 38 kuai – $10.50. When inquiring at the station how many days the trip would last, we received only the reassurance that however many it did take, the price would be the same. I found this particularly uncomforting.

By noon we were straining over high mountains of snow and ice. My thermometer hovered around 0 degrees, but the wind chill was fierce. The woman in front of me had progressed from retching to a comatose state that was frighteningly similar to death. I supposed this was in reaction to the altitude, a malady to which people who lived in the Turfan Depression no doubt were especially susceptible.

Around one o'clock we stopped for lunch at a bleak mountain outpost reeking of diesel fuel. A group of Hans played pool on a rough table outside the blockhouse restaurant. The players were in their twenties and wore high-heeled boots and scarves jauntily thrown over their shoulders. The table was a piece of green plywood balanced imperfectly on a pair of sawhorses. It had a hole in each corner but no pockets under the holes; several urchins scrambled for the ball whenever a shot was sunk, scurrying under the table legs with an efficiency worthy of the best ball boys at Wimbledon. The players chewed sunflower seeds and struck exaggerated poses between shots.

The restaurant served a delicious brown noodle in a thick gravy with onions and lamb fat. Outside, I bought some cookies in a rough cardboard box loosely stapled together. The cookies had no taste whatsoever. As an experiment, I broke off a piece of the box and chewed on it. While the textures were slightly different, the taste was indistinguishable.

All afternoon we passed through oasis towns, jumbles of mud

huts clinging together for support. Snow covered everything; this was a surprise. Fran said it looked like the Arctic, a desert Arctic, and that captured it well.

The Uighur women all wore brightly coloured scarves wrapped mummy-style around their head for warmth. I would have done the same except my scarf had fallen into a pool of vomit.

By late afternoon we had moved from the mountains to a flat, high plain. The road was smoother but icier and more treacherous. We crept along, surging occasionally up to 20 mph. I tried to read *Hindoo Holiday* by J. R. Ackerly in hope that the stories of tropical India would raise my body temperature by sympathetic association. But the bus shook so much reading was a struggle. I gave up and tried to think of Mississippi summers. That worked a little better.

As it began to get dark, we pulled into Korla where we were to stop for the night. Before reaching the inn, however, we stopped at a repair yard. For a long time, the mechanic who'd travelled with us from Turpan banged away under the bus. The yard was full of crumpled buses, obvious relics of hideous collisions. They stood as reminders of previous failed repair jobs.

Finally we pulled away and travelled across town to an inn. On the way the conductress got off and said, 'See you at seven.' But the driver interrupted, asserting we were to leave at six. The conductress nodded and turned around to face the passengers and said, loudly, 'OK, see you at seven,' then got off.

The inn was in a walled compound surrounded by food stands. Fires flared in the darkness, and donkey carts moved down the dirt street. It all felt medieval.

A Han behind a glass counter dispersed room numbers like a drill sergeant. Everyone lined up to get their room assignment and a battered metal tin of hot water for washing. The place stank of sweat and mould. Behind us in line, the woman who had been vomiting all day on the bus began to vomit on the floor.

'The room is only three yuan,' Mark said. 'Seventy-five cents.'

'Overpriced,' I muttered.

'Don't worry,' Fran said. 'Today was the worst day. I'm sure of it.'

JEFF GREENWALD

# THE SIZE OF THE WORLD

THE GENERICALLY named Canal slices into the heart of metropolitan Dubai, jiggling the lights of five-star hotels and churning the sodium street lamps into golden tea. Sony and Pepsi signs toss jazzy neon from nearby buildings, lending strolling lovers a Venusian glow. A broad green park separates the channel from the downtown noise and bustle, but the smells of frying fish and Russian perfume carry.

The heat of the day had receded, and the air was still and warm. Spilled popcorn lay strewn on the paved pedestrian corniche. Shahid and I walked slowly, enjoying the oasis of calm. Along the edge of the canal, worn wooden ships bobbed against the dock with soft crunching sounds. Crewmen's laundry hung limply on the rails; from inside the boats came the glow of battery-powered televisions, or the crackle of radio static. Late dinners sizzled on a few of the decks, the sharp smells of cumin and coriander – those eccentric cousins of the carrot – commingling with drifts of shit and diesel.

Shahid knew the boats well; well enough, at least, to deduce which of them might be bound for Karachi. Every third or fourth seemed a likely candidate, and I would bide my time on a bench while he climbed aboard and negotiated with the sailors. After an hour of this he'd found a possibility; a fishing boat leaving for Pakistan in about five days. I was grateful, but my enthusiasm was tempered by the knowledge that those five days would finally extinguish my dim, but still tenacious, Mount Kailas hopes.

We were hungry and tired, but I urged Shahid to try one more time. After bypassing half a dozen ramshackle ferries – 'No good for Karachi,' he explained – we came to the last one in line. Beyond it the canal widened, disappearing into the oil-slicked waters of the Persian Gulf.

I popped open a Coke while my companion climbed on board. Fifteen minutes later he reappeared, clutching a slip of paper.

'They will not go to Karachi,' Shahid announced. 'But a friend of this captain, he must be going.'

'When?'

'Tonight. Unless he has already left . . .'

A burst of adrenaline zapped my spine. 'Already left? Oh no . . . Which boat? Where?'

'Not here.' Shahid squinted at the paper. 'The boat is the *Fateh Al Khair*. Captain Hussain. It is docked across the city, at the Jabah Ali port. We must take a car . . .'

We jogged toward Nassar Square. A ferret-faced oil company executive and his 'date' – a Slavic call girl with industrial-size breasts – fell back in astonishment as I shot between them and into their waiting cab, pulling the gleeful Shahid with me.

'American way!' he chortled as we roared off. 'Indiana Jones! I like it very much.'

The *Fateh Al Khair* had not yet left. Shahid found Captain Hussain – a roly-poly sea dog in a soiled yellow caftan – wolfing down french fries in the dockside greasy spoon and watching, with childlike fascination, a rock video of Henry Rollins performing 'I'm a Liar' on MTV. The captain, as advertised, spoke no English, but with the help of Shahid and a world map I made my intentions clear. There followed a short dialogue between the two Pakistanis.

'He will help you,' Shahid announced. 'The crossing will take three days, if good weather.' He glanced at his watch. 'They will leave at four o'clock. In four hours. You must meet the captain here, and he will tell the police to stamp your passport. If you are late, even one minute late, they will go without you. You agree?'

I nodded. 'How much will I pay for my passage?'

'You will give as you wish,' Shahid relayed. 'But there is no need to give anything. He will help you because he is a good man. A good man, and a good Muslim.' Shahid and the captain clasped hands. 'Four in the morning. The captain says if you need anything for the trip, you must buy it now.'

We got back to town at 1 a.m. After buying Shahid dinner (Dubai never sleeps) and thanking him profusely I shopped like mad, purchasing everything I might need for three days on an open deck: sunscreen, lip balm, a straw hat, a towel, sandalwood soap, mosquito repellent, breath mints, two cartons of State Express 555 cigarettes (for the crew), a dozen AA batteries (for the OmniBook) and a case of root beer soda (for me). Repacking my Endless Journey, which lay gutted on my untouched bed at the Salalah Hotel, I made an awful discovery; ten minutes later I was standing in a musty alley, knocking frantically on the shuttered door of the luckless washerwoman who had consented to have my clothes cleaned and dried by next day noon. I brought the dripping load back to the Salalah, stuffed it in my pack and, at 3 a.m. sharp, hailed a cab for the ride back to Jabah Ali.

Captain Hussain was as good as his word. He signed me through emigration and, using the hand gestures that would be our sole means of communication for the entire crossing, directed me to his boat.

The wooden ferries anchored along the Jabah Ali dock lay four deep. The *Fateh Al Khair*, trimmed to sail, was on the outermost edge. It was an athletic effort to wrestle my pack and provisions across the railings, over the cargo and between the sleeping crewmen of the three intermediate boats; a task made no easier by the pitch-darkness or the dozens of cat-size rats and rat-size roaches that scurried underfoot. I boarded awash in sweat, gasping for breath and filthy as a junkyard dog.

It was difficult to get a good look at the barge, but its funkiness was beyond dispute. On the wooden deck, some fifty feet long by twenty feet wide, a dozen used cars and two new HiAce Super Custom vans were lashed down for transport to Pakistan. Above the aft deck loomed a one-room wheelhouse, reached by a wooden ladder. The toilet consisted of two naked planks, separated by a narrow gap, jutting from the stern. Hussain's nine-man crew lay strewn like casualties across the deck and in the wheelhouse, snoring on rough blankets.

The deck was crawling with cockroaches, but the real problem – the only problem – was that there was no room for me to lie down. In a last gasp of lateral thinking I opened the sliding side door of the nearest van and crawled gratefully inside. There, on cushions of cunningly whipped petroleum, I slept.

## UNPLUGGED

It was unimaginable that, beyond the tiny stage of our boat, somewhere over the gunmetal-grey waters of the Persian Gulf (or, by Day 2, the Gulf of Oman), the world was still happening. Israel and the PLO were signing a peace pact; Nelson Mandela was about to be sworn in as president of South Africa; graffiti artist Michael Fay was getting his ass whipped in Singapore. By night, as I lay curled in my dormant vehicular nest, Girl Scouts sold cookies in Wisconsin; Mexicans celebrated Cinco de Mayo; Winona Ryder put on her lipstick. Planet Earth rolled through space, circling its sun at sixty-seven thousand miles per hour, and it was jam-packed with creatures doing funny, mysterious things.

I spent my mornings and afternoons – all the daylight hours, in fact – propped on cushions in the wheelhouse, reading books or typing on my miraculous battery-powered OmniBook as Captain Hussain (whose rank, paradoxically, seemed to release him from any shred of responsibility) hibernated noisily upon his bunk. As I finished each of the novels I'd brought (Pynchon, Asimov, Maugham, le Carré) I would throw it ceremoniously off the stern, watching it bob briefly before sinking into the loam of the Gulf. Pynchon, I thought, would particularly appreciate this burial at sea; there was something poetic about *Vineland* dissolving into the notorious waterway, which I can nevermore think of as anything but alphabet soup.

It was upon the *Fateh Al Khair* that I first experienced the infinite delight of the bucket bath, taken in my tattered red Calvin Kleins behind the leering yellow shade of a secondhand Caterpillar bulldozer. The broad plastic splash bowls of tepid water were a holy baptism, rinsing off my Arabian week of accumulated sweat, atomised sand, factor 15 sunscreen, 100 percent DEET insect spray, primal fear, belly-button lint, fish oil, machine grease, powdered rust, spilled pineapple juice, mosquito hoofprints, chapati flour, toe jam, melted chocolate and loose grey hairs. I took these baths in the heat of the day, making myself scarce as the more devout members of the all-Muslim crew rolled out their woven straw mats for their own call to prayer. Hidden behind my bulldozer, self-consciously semi-naked, I watched their elaborate choreography of devotion. Each fifteen-minute meditation included a ritual of standing, bowing, cupping the hands behind the ears, extending the palms to receive an invisible liquid sacrament and, finally, washing the blessed ether over their dark, pious faces.

There was no mess. The meals, cooked in a wind-screened corner of the deck and served 'buffet-style', were hideous, but I ate them with good appetite, chasing away the boldest roaches and swallowing prophylactic doses of Pepto-Bismol afterward. I took up smoking, limiting my intake to three cigarettes a day: one at ten, one at two, and one just after sunset. And I shat in terror, once every morning at seven, clinging with both hands to the thick but fraying rope that, dangling damply from the ferry's stern, was all that kept me from following my books into the Gulf

The language barrier precluded intimacy with the crew, but a quiet cordiality prevailed. I was treated with unflagging courtesy. By our third day at sea I knew most of the sailors by name. There was Salim Mohammed, the navigator, who looked like a Pakistani version of Neil Young and wandered the decks in black nylon socks; Bahadin Kera Ibrahim, a tall, unsmiling black man who reminded me of a character from a Conrad story; and Ali Abdul Shaktar, second mate, whose teeth were stained crimson from years of chewing *pan*. First Mate Yaakov could always be recognised by his signature blue cap, while Ahmed Allah Rakha, the bosun, chain-smoked and had the laconic round eyes of a frog. The only one who seemed to resent my presence on board was Muhammed Ali, the cook, who found himself with an additional mouth to feed. On the afternoon of our fourth day at sea, when we ran out of food entirely, this ceased to be a problem.

And it was during the fourth evening of that long, exquisitely dull cruise, sitting on the bridge in the moonless sloshing dark, that I realised, with a start: *we had no radio*.

No radio! No flare! No way to signal for help, to alert even the nearest passerby if – as has been known to happen on large bodies of water – our luck went savagely awry. If something were to go wrong on the *Fateh* there would be no hope at all of calling upon the forces that be for a safe, speedy rescue. No radio! And, tied to the roof of the wheelhouse, only a tiny rubber raft, which, when I examined it closely, had the words 'Not To Be Used as a Life Preserver' emblazoned on its blubbery side.

In droll anguish I turned to the captain – dozing off to Hindi show tunes on a leather-encased transistor radio – and inquired, with a flurry of sign language, what we would do if there was a problem. Hussain smiled – a beatific, submissive Islamic smile – and simply waved his hands, right over left, horizontally, like cards being shuffled and returned to the deck. Right then and there I realised that, for the very first time on my entire global pilgrimage, I was truly and utterly Unwired. There was no stream of radio waves, no electromagnetic impulse, no vibrating string or even a smoke signal to link us with the World At Large.

Thus I found myself, after fifteen years of travel, finally able to answer a question that had stumped me eight months earlier at the Third Annual Book Passage Travel Writers' Conference. This, right here, was 'the single most remote spot' I had ever visited: the blue-trimmed wheelhouse of the *Fateh Al Khair*, with Mr Ibrahim at the wheel, morose Salim the navigator sitting at the foot of his usurped (by me) sleeping platform and the rotund Captain Hussain lounging in one of those vaguely yogic subcontinental postures with a Rothman's filter king dangling between his fingers and a pinch of snuff tucked beneath his lip.

There was nothing around us but water, comic-book blue, unbroken save for the very occasional flying fish or the smokelike silhouette of a distant tanker. Anything could happen; and if it did we would die, finally and anonymously, having for all intents and purposes (as my friend Pico Iyer might say) 'fallen off the map'.

By the late morning of Day 5 I knew we were in trouble. We'd left Dubai with enough fuel to last about 100 hours; come noon, we would have been at sea for 104. Land was nowhere in sight.

Ali Abdul Shaktar spied a fishing boat, and we changed course to intercept. It took us more than an hour to reach it, but choppy seas forbid an exchange of personnel. Any confidence I still maintained in Salim evaporated as I heard him – and one needed no Urdu for this – bellowing for directions to Karachi. The half-naked seamen on the fishing skiff pointed in three separate directions, arguing amongst themselves. Bahadin Kera Ibrahim, usually cool as a cucumber, broke into a sweat. The captain, acting on executive authority, lay down with his arm over his eyes.

Salim and the skiff's captain yelled back and forth, establishing something or other, and we hung a left.

Four hours later we accosted another trawler and, hearkening their unanimous counsel, hove 60 degrees to the right. It was five in the afternoon. We had by now run out of drinking water, and I was rationing root beer to the crew. Captain Hussain snored soundly, the stuffed tiger he had bought for his grandson tucked beneath his head.

The sun set. I sat atop my bulldozer, gazing at the evening star and flicking ashes into the sea. At any moment I expected to hear the death rattle of our engine, swallowing its last gulp of diesel and dooming us to slow extinction. What I heard instead was the voice of Ali Abdul Shaktar – old eagle eyes himself – hooting victoriously from the wheel. Strung between the inky sea and indigo sky, Karachi glittered on the horizon.

The *Fateh Al Khair* gagged and sputtered as we entered the harbour, stalling twice before reaching a berth. We had been at sea 112 hours – two days longer than the initial estimate. No sooner had we docked than hundreds of mosquitoes descended upon the boat, eager to graze on our sun-ripened limbs. The cockroaches and rats, sensing our evacuation, reappeared in force, boldly scrambling over the empty food stores and into the dry water barrel. Ibrahim, Salim and the other crewmen bagged their gear and, one by one, abandoned ship for the buses and taxis that would take them back to their families.

I put away my computer, retrieved my backpack and bid a less than fond farewell to the HiAce van that had served as my nest. A generous tip for our narcoleptic captain was folded into my shirt pocket. Every square inch of my skin was itching to get off that boat. Tonight, my first night in Asia, I would go for broke: an air-conditioned taxi, a five-course meal and a first-class hotel with a sauna and spa. Yes! Yes! I grabbed the cook's hands and danced a little jig, unable to believe it was over.

I was about to step over the railing and make my way to shore when the captain, more animated than I'd ever seen him, ran over and grabbed my arm.

'No, no, no!' he said.

'No, no, no!' echoed the remaining crewmen.

I looked at them as if they were crazy. It took twenty minutes of charades before I understood: Immigration was closed for the night. The officers would return at eleven the next morning. Until then I was confined, by letter of law, to the boat.

## DERVLA MURPHY

# FULL TILT
## Ireland to India on a Bicycle

ANOTHER DAY of incredible, unforgettable and indescribable beauty, plus our highest climb yet – 10,380 feet over the Shibar Pass; I felt like a fly going up a wall.

At breakfast this morning Mohammad tried to persuade me to go by truck as he simply didn't believe a cycle could be got over the Shibar but when I reached the foot of the pass I was very glad I hadn't agreed to his kind suggestion. At the moment there is heavy traffic on this route because Afghanistan and Pakistan are not on speaking terms and their frontier is closed, so that many of the goods which would normally be imported via Karachi and the Khyber Pass are coming from Russia via Mazar-i-Sharif. But this track was never meant to be a grand trunk road and the sight of grossly overloaded and mainly 'home-made' trucks negotiating these fantastic hairpin bends, with inches between the outer wheels and a 1,000-foot drop, made me sweat with vicarious terror – and thank God that it was only vicarious as I pushed Roz up, keeping close to the cliffside. In fact, the climb wasn't as stiff as I had anticipated, because the foot of the pass is itself about 7,000 feet above sea level; yet over the last thousand feet I did notice the effects of the altitude – shortness of breath and aching calf-muscles. But it was worth it all to rise gradually from that fertile, warm valley to the still, cold splendour of the snow-line, where the highest peaks of the Hindu Kush crowd the horizon in every direction and one begins to understand why some people believe that gods live on mountain tops.

There's an astounding change on this northern side of the range. Within a few miles the whole landscape has altered from early summer to late winter; trees are almost bare, grass and wheat are just beginning to show and the temperature is many degrees lower.

The downward gradient is much less severe and at one point the road goes through a glorious narrow gorge of red-brown cliffs; these are so close, so high and so sheer that standing between them, looking up, one has the sensation of being a midget dropped into some ruggedly built edifice with a slight crack in the roof.

It was at the end of this gorge that disaster hit Roz; she suffered two vicious rips in the back tyre and I doubt if they can be patched. The road is excruciating but personally I've got used to the feeling of being dislocated in every joint at one bump and relocated at the next. However, it's different for poor Roz and today's calamity was my fault; I let her go too fast down the pass. This was because of the back brake again giving trouble so that the alternative to cycling too fast was walking, and when you've walked up to 10,380 feet you don't feel much like walking down. At this stage it was 5.15 pm and we were some twenty miles from Bamian, near the junction of the Mazar–Bamian road where there is a tiny village called Bulola. I asked about a bus and one was pointed out as going to Bamian 'in a few minutes', so Roz was loaded up and I sat in. My other buses were luxurious compared with this one. The floor was covered in sheep and goat droppings and the steering-wheel was held together with sticking-plaster – a device not calculated to soothe one's nerves on a journey in this terrain. We finally set off at 6.20 pm, by which time I was frozen stiff – it had been raining hard and there was no glass in the windows, as usual – after sitting patiently watching huge piles of hides being roped together and tied to the roof till the whole rickety contraption looked gruesomely top-heavy. And just before our departure nine men had climbed up and settled down on top of the hides, wrapping themselves in their huge rugs.

About two miles beyond Bulola the engine broke down; it was

now dark and raining, and the repairs, during which the headlights were put out of order, took very nearly an hour. At 7.30 pm we resumed the journey up and over a 10,000-foot pass on a corkscrew 'road', barely wide enough for one vehicle, with sheer drops which I could imagine, but happily not see, as there was no light. Then quite soon there *was* light – lots of it – when the daily spring thunderstorm began. For several minutes lightning was continuous – not flashes as we know them, but glaring sheets of blue illumination, revealing gaunt peaks on one side and sickening ravines on the other; yet it was all so beautiful and awe-inspiring that one simply forgot to be afraid. The thunder reverberating in the mountains was deafening – peal after peal, the echoes of each being drowned in the crash of the next. With all this came gusts of gale-force wind carrying enormous hailstones which took the skin off my nose where they struck it as I sat next to the window-that-wasn't. There are limits even to Afghan toughness and when this demonstration started the bus stopped for the nine men on the roof to come below. As the 'inside' was already overcrowded beyond belief this meant that I had three children on my lap for the rest of the journey; I had only one two-year-old at the beginning. We waited for about fifteen minutes until the worst was over because to attempt to negotiate that winding track, with the driver intermittently dazzled by lightning would have been suicidal. (To my mind the whole trip wasn't far short of suicidal anyway.) Yet what an experience to see a landscape, dramatic in itself, under such melodramatic conditions – like some inspired choreographer's setting for Faust.

Soon after we had restarted a melodrama of a different kind began. The system on these privately owned buses is that the owner-driver's assistant, usually an adolescent known as a *bacha*, collects the fares during the journey. The bacha now asked twelve afghanis from everyone and a number of passengers protested that ten had been agreed on before the start. Hell then broke loose and while I was bundling the children under the seat an infuriated tribesman, brandishing his rifle, climbed over me, trying to get at the driver; the bacha pushed him, and he fell backwards, striking me a frightful blow on the ribs with the rifle-butt. I looked round to see a terrifying forest of rifle-barrels behind me – terrifying because in a jolting bus I imagined them going off accidentally; but of course these men know exactly what they are doing with their triggers, if not with their butts, and nothing of the sort happened. The unarmed bacha continued his heroic defence of the driver, the bus stopped yet again, the driver got out and stood grasping *his* gun and refusing to go another yard until everyone had paid their twelve afghanis and I hastily produced mine, vaguely hoping to set a good example. But I was completely ignored while the verbal battle raged and everyone fingered his trigger menacingly as though it wouldn't be verbal much longer; the angry shouts of all concerned almost drowned both the thunder and the hiss of the hail slashing down. Finally one of the passengers threatened to smash the inside light with his rifle-butt. Then a compromise of eleven afghanis was accepted, whereupon the driver resumed his seat and off we went again. This time – rather to my astonishment – we kept on going, at some 15 mph, until reaching Bamian, where Roz and I were decanted in total darkness and I was told that the hotel lay on my left. As I was switching on Roz's light a policeman appeared and almost wept with joy when he saw me – he'd been expecting me hours earlier. He had a storm-lantern and led me on a mile-long walk up a very steep hill to the hotel; we were halfway up when we encountered a car, stuck in deep, loose gravel and being pushed by two softly swearing men. Afghanistan's tourist trade is so flourishing that after a few weeks in the country most tourists are on christian name terms with each other, so I yelled 'Hi, what's wrong?' having recognised three very nice Indians I'd met in Kabul. They said that after the 140 miles from Kabul everything that could go wrong with a car was wrong and now they just wanted to get her as far as the hotel, to avoid leaving her unguarded all night. So Roz was dropped by the wayside and the policeman and I added our pushes, during which operation I began to suspect that my lowest right rib has been fractured by the rifle butt. When we eventually got the unfortunate machine over the crest of the hill the policeman said that he'd go back to the village as I had found friends and then, having retrieved Roz, I walked on with two of the Indians, who had stayed out of the car to save it extra weight. We were trotting along, numb with cold and exchanging our harrowing experiences of the road, when a blood-curdling yell halted us and we found ourselves looking down the barrel of a rifle held by a very young soldier. We gave a chorus of little yelps of terror and said 'Hotel! Hotel! Tourist's Hotel!' But the sentry wasn't at all sure that three strangers – one with a bicycle and two without luggage – coming suddenly out of the black, cold night, could be genuine tourists, so he kept us covered until another soldier had examined our passports. This second lad then led us to the hotel, some two hundred yards away from what is apparently a military barracks.

It was depressing, if not altogether surprising, to discover that here there was (a) no food or drink of any description, (b) no light, (c) no water, (d) no heating and (e) only one thin blanket on each bed. As we were now 8,550 feet above sea level (e) was not funny. I had coffee and sugar and bread with me and the boys had some tinned sausages and pineapples so we scraped together a meal of sorts by the light of oil-lamps borrowed from the military, making coffee with the boys' emergency water supply. (The side-splitting part of this story is that Bamian Hotel is listed as Luxury, Grade A!) Then we raided a vast number of empty bed-rooms and accumulated six blankets each; I am now sitting up in bed swathed in my six, with numb hands and feet and a howling gale blowing through the loose window-frame. But I suppose I should be grateful for glass in the windows . . .

WILLIAM DALRYMPLE

# IN XANADU
## A Quest

**T**HE DISADVANTAGES of travelling with a busload of stoned Uigurs only became apparent later. An hour after sunrise the early winter winds began to blow and by noon they had turned into quite respectable sandstorms. The windows were shut and everyone waited to see what would happen. Polo's *The Travels* contains descriptions of many of the horrors of the desert, but does not mention sandstorms. This is surprising as the *buran* of the Taklimakan are some of the most ferocious of any desert in the world. Of the descriptions of *buran* left by those who experienced them, none is as evocative as the much-quoted passage in von Le Coq's *Buried Treasures of Chinese Turkestan*:

> Quite suddenly the sky grows dark . . . a moment later the storm bursts with appalling violence. Enormous masses of sand, mixed with pebbles, are forcibly lifted up, whirled around and dashed down on man and beast; the darkness increases and strange clashing noises mingle with the roar and howl of the storm. The whole happening is like hell let loose . . .

Nothing quite as bad as von Le Coq's buran hit us, but as the wind increased in strength the sand from the dunes began to drift onto the road. At first this simply slowed us down, but gradually it began to make the going almost impossible. The bus finally drew to a halt in front of a huge drift thirty miles outside Keriya. The driver covered his mouth with a rag and disappeared outside with a shovel. A handful of the more *compos mentis* Uigurs and I went out to help him; the rest stayed in the bus puffing at their reefers. We shovelled away at the sand and placed wooden sleepers under the wheels to give the tyres some purchase. It worked. After an hour of hard labour the bus moved on, but drew to a halt only five miles further up the road. Again we all got out and shovelled.

The rest of that day was spent edging forward in this manner. At six the sun set over the distant Kunlun mountains, darkening the vast emptiness of the desert. Through the rattling of the bus came the quiet murmur of the Muslims saying their evening prayers. It was nearly midnight when we arrived at Niya.

The caravanserai was filthy, cold and had no food, but neither, thankfully, did it have any Public Security guards. We slept like children, but only until five o'clock. To keep ahead of the police we knew we had to be off before dawn. We also thought it wiser to change our transport. If the Keriya police had telegraphed forward to Charchan, the Public Security there would be expecting us on the bus. We guessed that we stood more chance of getting through travelling by truck. So, feeling ill and exhausted, we tramped around the different caravanserai dormitories looking for a driver who was leaving immediately, heading in the right direction and prepared to take us with him. Only one filled all these criteria: as at Khotan, we set off into the desert on top of a pile of coal. To mark the occasion we wore for the first time the 'disguises' we had bought in Keriya. Mine consisted of a Mao suit topped by a green Uigur skullcap; Louisa wore a printed dress and a white veil. From front-on, in broad daylight, neither disguise fooled anyone. Indeed on several occasions they caused hysterical peals of laughter from Uigurs who otherwise might never have noticed us. Nevertheless we thought that the 'disguises' did look vaguely convincing from the back. If ever we came to a checkpoint, we planned to fall forward on our faces and pretend to be asleep. Only the most officious guard would be rude enough to wake a sleeping couple, or so, at any rate, we hoped.

The next two days were exhausting. The constant worry of

being detected, occasional pangs of hunger and thirst, the physical effort of digging ourselves out of sand dunes, the daytime heat and the extreme night-time cold, all these different strains began to take their toll. Particularly unpleasant was the aggressive old man with whom we shared our coal slag. Our relationship got off to a bad start on the first day when, during a mid-morning *cay* stop, I blew my nose in his presence. For this unforgivable *faux pas* I earned myself a violent torrent of abuse. It appears that my crime was twofold: firstly blowing my nose while he was drinking, secondly using a handkerchief. Apparently polite Uigur etiquette demands that one walks away from any imbibing company, raises one's left hand to the ridge of one's nose and blows heartily through the nostrils, aiming to discharge the deposit onto the ground. Any overhang should then be wiped away, and the hand then cleaned on the shirt front. This was certainly how the old man approached the problem. It was on this same *cay* stop that my false front tooth finally fell out. This had a disproportionately lowering effect on my morale. It was now four days since my razor blades had been stolen and the combination of an unshaven yet unbearded face, a weatherworn visage and a gap-toothed smile was clearly an unpleasant one. It was several days before I next saw a mirror and was able to take in the full horror of it myself, but its effects on those around me was immediately obvious. It was about this time that little Uigur children began running away from me, screaming and shrieking for their parents.

That night we reached Charchan. Outside the caravanserai we ate the best kebabs in the world, then slunk quickly off to bed before our 'disguises' caused a riot. Long into the night we could hear the shrieks of laughter outside. Neither of us could sleep. A day exposed to the full glare of the desert sun had given us both bad sunburn, while the night chill was unbearable. We lay awake in our coal-grimed clothes, at once burning and shivering, a combination that was as unpleasant as it was unusual. We were up and waiting for the truck driver when he appeared at four-thirty the following morning.

The strain was now really beginning to show. We had been on the move for nearly a week and in that time had only one full night's sleep. Louisa was silent and irritable; I had sunk into a state of exhausted, toothless gloom. We had diarrhoea. Our clothes were torn and we were both filthy: neither of us had washed since Keriya. I was a terrible sight; poor Lou looked a little better but felt much worse. The colour had gone from her cheeks and she had ceased to take trouble with her appearance; for the first time she was beginning to look a little dishevelled. The next morning, after another sleepless night in another filthy caravanserai, she finally reached the end of her endurance. The coal truck left Waxari before dawn. Shortly afterwards she said: 'I think that I am going to be sick,' then was, several times. We arrived at the oasis of Charchalik about nine in the morning. There she announced that she was quite simply incapable of going on.

'If I spend one more minute on this truck,' she said quietly but very firmly, 'I will die.'

We took a bedroom from the club-footed caravanserai keeper. There we ordered a basin of hot water, then washed, dried and lay on our beds wondering how long it would be before the police came to hear of our arrival. They heard very quickly. At quarter past ten there was a knock on the door. Lou was asleep so I got up to open it. Outside stood two Public Security guards.

We were fined and made to sign a confession but we were not sent back. We had got far enough to make it more effort than it was worth. Instead, the next day, we were bundled into a police Jeep and deported northwards out of the security zone to the town of Korla near Turfan. There, still under arrest, we were made to buy tickets to Peking and seen on to the train.

We had got as far as the border of the desert of Lop, what we learned later was the Chinese nuclear testing ground. It was this discovery that gave our final day in Charchalik a special poignancy.

After the police discovered us in the morning, they locked us up in our hotel room, perhaps for lack of anywhere better to put us. That evening they let us out to eat supper. Lou did not feel like eating, so I was taken on my own to a shabby restaurant owned by a deaf mute. As he was possibly the only other person for five hundred miles who was unable to speak or understand either Chinese or Uigur I felt a certain bond between us and lingered in his café, toying with a bowl of chop suey, while the Public Security guard waited by the door. It was only after half an hour that I began to notice how many other cripples there were in the restaurant. It seemed that there was not a single healthy person in the town: some had terrible contorted limbs and strange disfiguring marks on their skin. A few were completely bald; others were thin and wasted. There can only be one explanation for this gathering in one small town. It must have been something to do with radiation from the testing ground. No wonder the police were so quick to deport us: we appeared to have stumbled across an oasis populated by mutants.

# THE MOON

# MEN FROM EARTH

WE WERE JUST 700 feet above the surface when Charlie gave us the final 'go', just as another 12 02 alarm flashed. Neil and I confirmed with each other that the landing radar was giving us good data, and he punched PROCEED into the keyboard. All these alarms had kept us from studying our landing zone. If this had been a simulation back at the Cape, we probably would have aborted. Neil finally looked away from the DSKY screen and out his triangular window. He was definitely not satisfied with the ground beneath us. We were too low to identify the landmark craters we'd studied from the *Apollo 10* photographs. We just had to find a smooth place to land. The computer, however, was taking us to a boulder field surrounding a 40-foot-wide crater.

Neil rocked his hand controller in his fist, changing over to manual command. He slowed our descent from 20 feet per second to only nine. Then, at 300 feet, we were descending at only three and a half feet per second. As *Eagle* slowly dropped, we continued skimming forward.

Neil still wasn't satisfied with the terrain. All I could do was give him the altimeter call-outs and our horizontal speed. He stroked the hand controller and descent-rate switch like a motorist fine-tuning his cruise control. We scooted across the boulders. At two hundred feet our hover slid toward a faster descent rate.

'Eleven forward, coming down nicely,' I called, my eyes scanning the instruments. 'Two hundred feet, four and a half down.

Five and a half down. One sixty . . .' The low-fuel light blinked on the caution-and-warning panel, '. . . quantity light.'

At 200 feet, Neil slowed the descent again. The horizon of the moon was at eye level. We were almost out of fuel.

'Sixty seconds,' Charlie warned.

The ascent engine fuel tanks were full, but completely separate from the descent engine. We had sixty seconds of fuel remaining in the descent stage before we had to land or abort. Neil searched the ground below.

'Down two and a half,' I called. The LM [Lunar Module] moved forward like a helicopter flaring out for landing. We were in the so-called dead man's zone, and we couldn't remain there long. If we ran out of fuel at this altitude, we would crash into the surface before the ascent engine could lift us back toward orbit. 'Forward. Forward. Good. Forty feet. Down two and a half. Picking up some dust. Thirty feet . . .'

Thirty feet below the LM's gangly legs, dust that had lain undisturbed for a billion years blasted sideways in the plume of our engine.

'Thirty seconds,' Charlie announced solemnly, but still Neil slowed our rate.

The descent engine roared silently, sucking up the last of its fuel supply. I turned my eye to the ABORT STAGE button. 'Drifting right,' I called, watching the shadow of a footpad probe lightly touching the surface. 'Contact light.' The horizon seemed to rock gently and then steadied. Our altimeter stopped blinking. We were on the moon. We had about twenty seconds of fuel remaining in the descent stage. Immediately I prepared for a sudden abort, in case the landing had damaged the *Eagle* or the surface was not strong enough to support our weight.

'Okay, engine stop,' I told Neil, reciting from the checklist. 'ACA out of detent.'

'Got it,' Neil answered, disengaging the hand control system. Both of us were still tingling with the excitement of the final moments before touchdown.

'Mode controls, both auto,' I continued, aware that I was

chanting the readouts. 'Descent engine command override, off. Engine arm, off . . .'

'We copy you down, *Eagle*,' Charlie Duke interrupted from Houston.

I stared out at the rocks and shadows of the moon. It was as stark as I'd ever imagined it. A mile away, the horizon curved into blackness.

'Houston,' Neil called, 'Tranquillity Base here. The *Eagle* has landed.'

It was strange to be suddenly stationary. Spaceflight had always meant movement to me, but here we were rock-solid still, as if the LM had been standing here since the beginning of time. We'd been told to expect the remaining fuel in the descent stage to slosh back and forth after we touched down, but there simply wasn't enough reserve fuel remaining to do this. Neil had flown the landing to the very edge.

'Roger, Tranquillity,' Charlie said, 'we copy you on the ground. You've got a bunch of guys about to turn blue. We're breathing again. Thanks a lot.'

I reached across and shook Neil's hand, hard. We had pulled it off. Five months and ten days before the end of the decade, two Americans had landed on the moon.

'It looks like a collection of just every variety of shapes, angularities, granularities, every variety of rock you could find . . .' I told Houston. Everyone wanted to know what the moon looked like. The glaring sunrise was directly behind us like a huge searchlight. It bleached out the colour, but the greys swam in from the sides of my window.

Charlie said there were 'lots of smiling faces in this room, and all over the world'.

Neil grinned at me, the strain leaving his tired eyes. I smiled back. 'There are two of them up here,' I told Charlie.

Mike's voice cut in much louder and clearer than Mission Control. 'And don't forget the one in the command module.'

Charlie told Mike to speak directly to us. 'Roger, Tranquillity Base,' Mike said. 'It sounded great from up here. You guys did a fantastic job.'

That was a real compliment coming from a pilot as skilled as Mike Collins.

'Thank you,' Neil said. 'Just keep that orbiting base ready for us up there now.'

We were supposed to do a little housekeeping in the LM, eat a meal and then try to sleep for seven hours before getting ready to explore the surface. But whoever signed off on that plan didn't know much psychology – or physiology, for that matter. We'd just landed on the moon and there was a lot of adrenaline still zinging through our bodies. Telling us to try to sleep *before* the EVA was like telling kids on Christmas morning they had to stay in bed until noon.

I decided to begin a ceremony I'd planned with Dean Woodruff, my pastor at Webster Presbyterian Church. He'd given me a tiny Communion kit that had a silver chalice and wine vial about the size of the tip of my little finger. I asked 'every person listening in, whoever and wherever they may be, to pause for a moment and contemplate the events of the past few hours, and to give thanks in his or her own way.' The plastic note-taking shelf in front of our DSKY became the altar. I read silently from Dean's Communion service – *I am the wine and you are the branches* . . . – as I poured the wine into the chalice. The wine looked liked syrup as it swirled around the sides of the cup in the light gravity before it finally settled at the bottom.

*Eagle*'s metal body creaked. I ate the tiny Host and swallowed the wine. I gave thanks for the intelligence and spirit that had brought two young pilots to the Sea of Tranquillity.

Suiting up for the moon walk took us several hours. Our PLSS backpacks looked simple, but they were hard to put on and tricky to operate. They were truly our life-support systems, with enough oxygen, cooling water, electrical power and radio equipment to keep us alive on the moon and in constant contact with Houston (via a relay in the LM) for four hours. On Earth, the PLSS and spacesuit combination weighed 190 pounds, but here it was only 30. Combined with my own body weight, that brought me to a total lunar-gravity weight of around 60 pounds.

Seven hours after we touched down on the moon, we depressurised the LM, and Neil opened the hatch. My job was to guide him as he backed out on his hands and knees on to the small porch. He worked slowly, trying not to jam his backpack on the hatch frame. When he reached the ladder attached to the forward landing leg, he moved down carefully.

The new capcom, Bruce McCandless, verified that we were doing everything correctly. Once Neil reached over and pulled a line to deploy the LM's television camera, Bruce said, 'We're getting a picture on the TV.'

'I'm at the foot of the ladder,' Neil said, his voice slow and precise. 'The LM footpads are only depressed in the surface about one or two inches.' The surface was a very fine-grain powder. 'I'm going to step off the LM now . . .'

From my window I watched Neil move his blue lunar overshoe from the metal dish of the footpad to the powdery grey surface.

'That's one small step for . . . man, one giant leap for mankind.'

Lunar gravity was so springy that coming down the ladder was both pleasant and tricky. I took a practice run at getting back up to that high first step, and then I hopped down beside Neil.

'Isn't that something?' Neil asked. 'Magnificent sight out here.'

I turned around and looked out at a horizon that dropped

steeply away in all directions. We were looking 'down sun', so there was only a black void beyond the edge of the moon. For as far as I could see, pebbles, rock fragments and small craters covered the surface. Off to the left, I could make out the rim of a larger crater. I breathed deeply, goose flesh covering my neck and face. 'Beautiful, beautiful,' I said. 'Magnificent desolation.'

Stepping out of the LM's shadow was a shock. One moment I was in total darkness, the next in the sun's hot floodlight. From the ladder I had seen all the sunlit moonscape beyond our shadow, but with no atmosphere, there was absolutely no refracted light around me. I stuck my hand out past the shadow's edge into the sun, and it was like punching through a barrier into another dimension. I moved around the legs of the LM to check for damage.

'Looks like the secondary strut has a little thermal effect on it right here, Neil,' I said, pointing to some engine burn on the leg.

'Yeah,' Neil said, coming over beside me. 'I noticed that.'

We were both in the sun again, our helmets close together. Neil leaned toward me and clapped his gloved hand on my shoulder. 'Isn't it fun?' he said.

I was grinning ear to ear, even though the gold visor hid my face. Neil and I were standing together on the *moon*.

# NOTES ON CONTRIBUTORS

EDWIN 'BUZZ' ALDRIN first took flight at the age of two, and eventually progressed to flying F86 jets in Korea before becoming involved in the Gemini and Apollo space projects. *Men from Earth* and *Return to Earth* deal with his experiences of travel beyond Earth; he is also the author of a science-fiction novel, *Encounter with Tiber*.

DEA BIRKETT is a British writer, journalist and broadcaster, who has been published on both sides of the Atlantic. Her first travel book, *Jella: from Lagos to Liverpool, A Woman at Sea in a Man's World*, won the Somerset Maugham Award. She lives in England.

ROLF BJELKE has been sailing to the Antarctic since 1989 aboard *Northern Light*, a 40-foot steel ketch he owns with his wife, Deborah Shapiro. Their goal was to sail from Sweden to the Antarctic Peninsula, where they would overwinter before returning home. *Time on Ice* is the story of that voyage.

MARIA COFFEY is a Canadian writer with a long list of books to her credit, including titles as diverse as *A Cat in a Kayak* and *Three Moons in Vietnam*. She is also the author of *Sailing Back in Time*.

TED CONOVER is a peripatetic journalist, having written books about the high-fashion skiing scene in Aspen, Colorado (*Whiteout*), and the problem of illegal Mexican immigration into the United

States (*Coyotes*), both named Notable Books of the Year by the *New York Times*. His latest book is *Newjack*, an account of his year-long experience as a prison guard at Sing Sing, New York's notorious maximum security prison.

WILLIAM DALRYMPLE was born in Scotland and brought up on the shores of the Firth of Forth. He wrote the highly acclaimed, award-winning bestseller *In Xanadu* when he was twenty-two. He lived for five years in India where he researched his second book, *City of Djinns*. Travel also forms the backdrop to his subsequent books, *From the Holy Mountain* and *The Age of Kali*.

ROBYN DAVIDSON was born in a country town in Queensland, Australia. Her decision to travel to central Australia, train her own camels and then explore the desert areas of the outback with them resulted in her first book, *Tracks*. She is also the author of *Desert Places*, which describes her experiences with nomads in India.

WHIT DESCHNER is a satirist of the first order, having penned his first book about kayaking, entitled *Does the Wet Suit You? Confessions of a Kayak Bum*. He has paddled on rivers around the world, and has gone on to become a novelist (*Burning the Iceberg*). When he isn't travelling, he lives in Oregon, where he runs a small book-publishing business, The Eddie Tern Press.

CHRIS DUFF has travelled over 14,000 miles by sea kayak, and in 1986 he became the first person to solo paddle the entire British Isles. He is a contributing author to *Seekers of the Horizon* and writes frequently for *Sea Kayaker* magazine. He lives in Port Angeles, Washington.

DAVID EWING DUNCAN is the author of five books, including *Pedaling the Ends of the Earth* and *Hernando De Soto*. He is also a television and documentary producer. His most recent books are *Calendar*, which traces the development of the modern-day calendar, and *Copernicus's Monster*. He lives in San Francisco.

JEFF GREENWALD was reared amongst the Long Island shopping malls but now makes his home in Oakland, California. His reflections of travel, science and the global community have appeared in newspapers, magazines and anthologies worldwide. He is also the author *Shopping for Buddhas and Mister Raja's Neighborhood.*

BRIAN HALL is an American writer who lives in Ithaca, New York. He is the author of *The Impossible Country: A Journey through the Last Days of Yugoslavia,* and two novels: *The Saskiad* and *Madeleine's World.*

ERIC HANSEN lives in San Francisco and has travelled through Australia, Asia and the Middle East. He has been jailed in three countries for travelling without permission. *Stranger in the Forest* won the 1991 Grand Prix de Voyage, and he is also the author of *Motoring with Mohammed* and *Orchid Fever.*

TONY HORWITZ is a Pulitzer Prize-winning journalist and author of *Baghdad without a Map.* After years of traipsing through war zones as a foreign correspondent, he returned to Virginia to find that his childhood obsession with the American Civil War had caught up with him. He happened to encounter those unusual characters who re-enact the war, and his book *Confederates in the Attic* is the result.

PICO IYER is a writer whose work has appeared in the *TLS,* the *New York Review of Books* and magazines on both sides of the Pacific and the Atlantic. His books include *Video Night in Kathmandu, Falling Off the Map, Cuba and the Night* and *Tropical Classical.* He now lives in Japan with the heroine of his *Lady and the Monk.*

MARK JENKINS is a well-published writer in the United States, where his stories on adventure travel and mountaineering appear frequently in *Outside* and *Backpacker,* among other popular magazines. He is also the author of *Off the Map: Bicycling across Siberia.* He lives in Laramie, Wyoming.

KEVIN KERTSCHER lives in Boston, Massachusetts. He is an independent film-maker; *Africa Solo* is his first book.

KATHERINE KIZILOS was born in Australia, and lives in Melbourne. She works as a journalist and has lived in Greece, where she has also travelled extensively.

GRAHAM MACKINTOSH, an Englishman, seems an unlikely candidate to walk the 3000-mile coast of Baja, California. He calls himself 'the most unadventurous person in the world', yet he eventually spent 500 days in the loneliest of deserts, providing the stories for his book *Into a Desert Place*. He lives in San Diego.

MALCOLM McCONNELL is an American author who has written on subjects far and wide: the recovery of the Titanic, the defection of a Soviet pilot, the invasion of Panama and the US Central Intelligence Agency. His latest book is *Into the Mouth of the Cat*.

TOM MILLER is the author of *On the Border: Portraits of America's Southwestern Frontier*. His most recent work is *Trading with the Enemy*, a firsthand tour of Cuba, describing his experiences drinking with bartenders who knew Hemingway, travelling with a baseball team and touring Guantanamo Bay.

GEOFFREY MOORHOUSE is a prominent – and prolific – British travel author. Among his eighteen books are such works as *Calcutta, To the Frontier* (which won the Thomas Cook Award for the best travel book of 1984) and *Sun Dancing: A Vision of Medieval Ireland*. His most recent books include *Sydney: The Story of a City* and *India Britannica: A Vivid Introduction to the History of British India*. In 1982 he was elected a Fellow of the Royal Society of Literature. He lives in North Yorkshire.

DERVLA MURPHY was born and still lives in Ireland. Her intrepid travels by bicycle and other means have been described in her many books, which include *One Foot in Laos*, *Eight Feet in the Andes*, *In Ethiopia with a Mule*, *Muddling through in Madagascar* and *On a Shoestring to Coorg*.

ERIC NEWBY was born and still lives in England. He sailed to Australia and back in the last great fleet of sailing ships; he worked in the world of high fashion; and was held as a POW in Italy in World War II. He also worked as Travel Editor of the *Observer*. He is the author of more than fifteen books, among them *A Short Walk in the Hindu Kush*, *Slowly Down the Ganges*, *Love and War in the Apennines* and *A Small Place in Italy*.

RORY NUGENT is an American explorer and zoologist. In *Drums along the Congo* he chronicled his adventures searching for the elusive Mokele-Mbembe, a dinosaur-like creature reported to live in the river. He is also the author of *The Search for the Pink-Headed Duck*, about his journey for an extinct species in the Himalaya.

REDMOND O'HANLON was born in England, where he still lives with his family. He was the natural history editor of the *TLS* for fifteen years, and is a Fellow of the Royal Geographical Society and the Royal Society of Literature. *Into the Heart of Borneo*, *In Trouble Again* and *Congo Journey* number among his books.

RICK RIDGEWAY is a renowned Everest mountaineer and was part of the first American team to climb K2. He is the author of *Seven Summits* and *The Last Step: The American Ascent of K2*, and has been involved in a number of climbing films, both as a climber and cameraman. He lives in Ojai, California.

ALASTAIR SCOTT is a well-travelled writer who has produced three books that cover the globe (*A Scot Goes South*, *A Scot Returns* and *Scot Free*). His latest book, *Native Stranger: A Journey in Familiar and Foreign Scotland*, is a return full-circle to his home country.

DEBORAH SHAPIRO is an expert on Antarctica, and the co-author of *Northern Light: One Couple's Epic Voyage from the Arctic to the Antarctic*. During the 28,000-nautical-mile trip (which took three years to complete), she and her husband, Rolf Bjelke, endured battering seas, treacherous ice flows and complete isolation while frozen at the bottom of the world.

JOE SIMPSON is an award-winning travel writer and a cult figure among mountaineering authors. His gripping memoirs, which describe harrowing climbs around the world, include *Dark Shadows Falling*, *Storms of Silence* and *This Game of Ghosts*. He lives in Sheffield, England.

STUART STEVENS is an American political consultant and the author of several whimsical travelogues, including *Malaria Dreams: An African Adventure*. In his latest book, *Feeding Frenzy*, he accepts the formidable challenge of dining in all twenty-nine of the Michelin three-star restaurants in Europe on consecutive nights.

MIKE STROUD, with Sir Ranulph Fiennes, made the first unassisted crossing of Antarctica in 1993, the longest polar journey in history. He is also the author of *Survival of the Fittest: Understanding Health and Peak Physical Performance*, a topic he understands better than most people.

PAUL THEROUX was born in Medford, Massachusetts. His first novel was published in 1967 and he has since written more than twenty books, both fiction and non-fiction. His numerous travel books include *The Great Railway Bazaar*, *Riding the Iron Rooster*, *The Happy Isles of Oceania* and *The Pillars of Hercules*.

# LONELY PLANET JOURNEYS

JOURNEYS is a unique collection of travel writing – published by the company that understands travel better than anyone else.

It is a series for anyone who has ever experienced – or dreamed of – the magical moment when they encountered a strange culture or saw a place for the first time. They are tales to read while you're planning a trip, while you're on the road or while you're in an armchair, in front of a fire.

These outstanding titles explore our planet through the eyes of a diverse group of international writers. JOURNEYS books catch the spirit of a place, illuminate a culture, recount an adventure, or introduce a fascinating way of life. They always entertain, and always enrich the experience of travel.

**'Lively, intelligent and varied . . . an important contribution to travel literature' – *Age (Melbourne)***

---

# LONELY PLANET UNPACKED

**Travel Disaster Stories**
***By Tony Wheeler and other Lonely Planet Writers***

Every traveller has a horror story to tell: lost luggage, bad weather, illness or worse. In this lively collection of travel disaster tales, Lonely Planet writers share their worst moments of life on the road.

From Kenya to Sri Lanka, from Brazil to Finland, from the Australian outback to India, these travellers encounter hurricanes, road accidents, secret police and nasty parasites. Reading these funny and frightening stories from the dark side of the road will make you think twice about a career as a travel writer!

**'Lonely Planet celebrates its road-stained wretches in . . . a collection of tales of delightful disaster'**
**– *Don George, Travel Editor, salon.com***

## DRIVE THRU AMERICA
### *Sean Condon*

If you've ever wanted to drive across the US but couldn't find the time (or afford the gas), *Drive Thru America* is perfect for you.

In his search for American myths and realities – along with comfort, cable TV and good, reasonably priced coffee – Sean Condon paints a hilarious road-portrait of the USA.

**'entertaining and laugh-out-loud funny'**
*– Alex Wilber, Travel editor, Amazon.com*

---

## SEAN & DAVID'S LONG DRIVE
### *Sean Condon*

Sean and David are young townies who have rarely strayed beyond city limits. One day, for no good reason, they set out to discover their homeland, and what follows is a wildly entertaining adventure that covers half of Australia.

**'a hilariously detailed log of two burned out friends'**
*– Rolling Stone*

**'a definitive Generation X road epic ... a wonderful read'**
*– Globe & Mail*

## SHOPPING FOR BUDDHAS
### *Jeff Greenwald*

In his obsessive search for the perfect Buddha statue in the backstreets of Kathmandu, Jeff Greenwald discovers more than he bargained for . . . and his souvenir-hunting turns into an ironic metaphor for the clash between spiritual riches and material greed. Politics, religion and serious shopping collide in this witty account of an enlightening visit to Nepal.

**'Greenwald's quest reveals more about modern Nepal . . . than writings that take themselves much more seriously'**
*– Chicago Tribune*

## THE OLIVE GROVE
### Travels in Greece
### *Katherine Kizilos*

Katherine Kizilos travels to fabled islands, troubled border zones and her family's village deep in the mountains. She vividly evokes breathtaking landscapes, generous people and passionate politics, capturing the complexities of a country she loves.

*The Olive Grove* tells of other journeys too: the life-changing journey made by the author's emigrant father; the migration of young Greeks to cities; and the tremendous impact of tourism on Greek society.

**'beautifully captures the real tensions of Greece'**
*– Sunday Times*

# THE LONELY PLANET STORY

Lonely Planet published its first book in 1973 in response to the numerous 'How did you do it?' questions Maureen and Tony Wheeler were asked after driving, busing, hitching, sailing and railing their way from England to Australia.

Written at a kitchen table and hand collated, trimmed and stapled, *Across Asia on the Cheap* became an instant local bestseller, inspiring thoughts of another book.

Eighteen months in South-East Asia resulted in their second guide, *South-East Asia on a shoestring*, which they put together in a backstreet Chinese hotel in Singapore in 1975. The 'yellow bible', as it quickly became known to backpackers around the world, soon became *the* guide to the region. It has sold well over half a million copies and is now in its 10th edition, still retaining its familiar yellow cover.

Today there are over 350 titles, including travel guides, walking guides, language kits and phrasebooks, travel atlases and travel literature. The company is the largest independent travel publisher in the world.

The emphasis continues to be on travel for independent travellers. Tony and Maureen still travel for several months of each year and play an active part in the writing, updating and quality control of Lonely Planet's guides.

They have been joined by over 80 authors and 400 staff at our offices in Melbourne (Australia), Oakland (USA), London (UK) and Paris (France). Travellers themselves also make a valuable contribution to the guides through the feedback we receive in thousands of letters each year and on our web site.

The people at Lonely Planet strongly believe that travellers can make a positive contribution to the countries they visit, both through their appreciation of the countries' culture, wildlife and natural features, and through the money they spend. In addition, the company makes a direct contribution to the countries and regions it covers. Since 1986 a percentage of the income from each book has been donated to ventures such as famine relief in Africa; aid projects in India; agricultural projects in Central America; Greenpeace's efforts to halt French nuclear testing in the Pacific; and Amnesty International.

**'I hope we send people out with the right attitude about travel. You realise when you travel that there are so many different perspectives about the world, so we hope these books will make people more interested in what they see.'**

*— Tony Wheeler*